# GOD'S
# FAMILY

Story Bible Series, Book 1

# GOD'S FAMILY

*Stories of God and His People: Genesis*

Retold by Eve MacMaster

Illustrated by James Converse

HERALD PRESS
Scottdale, Pennsylvania
Kitchener, Ontario
1981

Library of Congress Cataloging in Publication Data

MacMaster, Eve, 1942-
  God's family.

  (Story Bible series; bk. 1)
  Summary: This first book of a series about God and
His people begins with the story of Creation, continues
through Adam and Eve, Noah, and Abraham, and concludes
with Joseph's enslavement in Egypt.
  1. Bible stories, English—O.T. Genesis. [1. Bible
stories—O.T. Genesis] I. Converse, James, ill.
II. Bible. O.T. Genesis. III. Title. IV. Series.
BS551.2.M296      222'.1109505      81-6551
ISBN 0-8361-1964-9 (pbk.)          AACR2

GOD'S FAMILY
Copyright © 1981 by Herald Press, Scottdale, Pa. 15683
    Published simultaneously in Canada by Herald Press,
    Kitchener, Ont. N2G 4M5
Library of Congress Catalog Card Number: 81-6551
International Standard Book Number: 0-8361-1964-9
Printed in the United States of America
Design: Alice B. Shetler

81 82 83 84 85 86 87 88 10 9 8 7 6 5 4 3 2 1

# Author's Note

*God's Family* is book 1 of the Herald Press Story Bible series. When finished, it will tell the complete story of God and his people as recorded in the Bible.

These stories were first written centuries ago in the Hebrew language to tell people of God's actions in human history. They have been translated and retold many times, because they're true stories about real people and how they came to be God's people.

Some of the stories are happy, and some are sad enough to make you cry. Some are serious and some are so funny you'll laugh out loud.

The Bible stories in this series are complete, adding little except a few historical and geographical explanations, and leaving out little except repetitions. I have tried to preserve the strong sense of story that adults as well as children enjoyed when the Bible was new.

Much work and love have gone into this project, and many of God's people have helped out along the way.

Bible professors George R. Brunk III, Ronald D. Guengerich, and G. Irvin Lehman, childhood curriculum and librarian specialists Elsie E. Lehman and A. Arlene Bumbaugh, and Choice Books executive Angie B. Williams have read the book in its early stages and offered valuable suggestions.

Paul M. Schrock, book editor at Herald Press, has given important advice and encouragement.

Sam, Tom, and Sarah MacMaster have "tested" the stories as they have been written.

Richard MacMaster has believed in the project from the beginning and made room for it in our family life. This one's for him.

*Eve MacMaster*
Bridgewater, Virginia

# Contents

## The Story of Joseph and His Brothers

## Maps

# Stories from the Beginning

# God Creates the World

*Genesis 1—2*

IN the beginning, there was God. Just God. There was nothing else—no people or animals, no earth or sun or stars, not even an empty sky. Before time began, God was. God never began, and no one made him. He always was.

At the beginning of time, God began to create. He created the stars, including our sun, and he created the planets, including our earth.

When God first made the earth, it was a dark and empty world, covered with water and thick black clouds. A mighty wind blew the clouds in a great storm across the water.

Then God spoke. He said, "Let there be light!"

Light came upon the earth. Sunlight began to break through the dark clouds and to shine upon the water.

God was pleased with the light. He separated it from the darkness, calling the light "day" and the darkness "night."

This was the first day on the earth.

Then God said, "Let there be sky above the earth!"

The clouds rose up above the surface of the water, and clear air formed a sky over the earth.

This was the second day.

Next God said, "Let the water under the sky come together in one place, so the dry land will appear!"

All the water came together and formed seas and oceans. The land that was under the water rose up and formed islands and continents, with hills and valleys and mountains.

God called the dry land "earth" and the water "seas," and he liked them very much.

Then God said, "Let all kinds of plants grow out of the ground, green plants and flowers, bushes and trees!"

Green plants began to grow and cover the land. Mosses and ferns and grass, flowers and bushes and trees filled the earth with fields and forests.

This was the third day.

Then God said, "Let the sun and the moon and the stars shine in the sky above the earth, to measure the days and the years, and to give light to the earth!"

The heavy dark clouds blew away and the sky was clear. The sun and the moon and the stars began to shine down upon the earth.

God saw that the earth was good.

This was the fourth day.

Next God said, "Let the seas be filled with all kinds of fish, and let birds fly in the sky above the earth!"

Large and small sea animals and all kinds of fish began to swim and live in the sea. All kinds of birds began to fly in the air.

God liked the fish and the birds very much.

This was the fifth day.

Then God said, "Let all kinds of animals live on the earth, wild animals and tame animals, animals that walk and animals that creep and crawl!"

Wild animals and tame animals, large animals and small animals began to live on the earth. They walked and hopped, crept and crawled in the valleys and on the mountains, in the fields and in the forests.

God was pleased with all of them.

Finally God said, "Now I'll make people! I'll make human beings different from the animals. They'll be like me, made in my image. And I'll put them in charge of all the animals."

He took a lump of soil from the ground and molded and shaped it into a man. Then he breathed life into the man's nostrils, and the man came alive.

God called the man "Adam," a name which means "mankind" or "human being."

Then God made a home for Adam. He planted an enormous garden in Eden, at a place where four rivers met to form one wide river. The garden was as large as a park, and the river ran through the middle of it.

God made all kinds of trees grow in the garden—flowering trees, shade trees, and fruit trees. In the middle of the garden he put a tree that was different from all the others—the tree of the knowledge of good and evil.

God took Adam and put him in the garden. He told Adam to take care of it, to plant the seeds and water the trees and flowers and pick the fruit and vegetables when they were ripe.

Then he explained something very important.

"You may eat any fruit that grows in this garden," God said, "except one. You must not eat fruit from the tree of the knowledge of good and evil, which grows in the middle of the garden. If you do, you will die."

Then God said, "It's not right for Adam to be alone. I'll give him a partner."

He brought all the animals to Adam, and he let the man name them. While God watched, Adam carefully looked at each animal. Then Adam gave each a name: goldfish and whale, robin and blue-bird, frog and pig and lion and on and on, until all the animals had names.

But none of them was a person like Adam; none of them could be his partner.

So then God put Adam to sleep. While he was sleeping, God took a rib bone from Adam's side and made it into a woman.

When Adam woke up, God brought the woman to him.

"At last!" said Adam. "Here's someone like me! A person, not an animal! She's just right to be my partner!"

Adam and the woman became the first husband and wife in the world. Adam called his wife "Eve," a name which means "living."

God blessed Adam and Eve. He told them, "I've made you, man and woman, in my image. You're like me. I've given you everything you need. I want you to have children and grandchildren and great-grandchildren, on and on, so the world will be filled with your family.

"I'm putting you in charge of all the fish and birds and animals in the world. I want you to take good care of them. I've given you fruit and grain and vegetables to eat, and I've made green plants to feed the animals."

God was pleased with the plants and animals and people that he had made. He looked at the beautiful world that he had given to Adam and Eve. It was perfect.

God finished making everything on the sixth day. On the next day he rested from his work. God blessed the seventh day and set it apart as a Sabbath, a special day for resting.

And then God rested.

# 2

# Adam and Eve Disobey God

*Genesis 3*

FOR a long time Adam and Eve lived happily in the garden of Eden. They enjoyed each other's company. They took good care of the animals and the garden. God often came to visit them and to talk with them. Everything was perfect.

Then something happened that changed all that.

In the garden lived a snake, the sliest and cleverest animal God had made. One day the snake asked Eve, "Is it true that God told you not

17

to eat any of the fruit that grows in this garden?"

"Oh, no," answered Eve. "We may eat any fruit we want to, except the fruit that grows on the tree in the middle of the garden. God told us not to eat the fruit of the tree of the knowledge of good and evil. If we eat it, or even touch it, we will die."

"That's not true," said the snake. "You won't die. God lied to you. He knows that if you eat it, you'll become as wise as he is."

Eve thought about that.

Then she walked slowly over to the middle of the garden. She looked at the tree of the knowledge of good and evil. How lovely it was! She looked at the ripe, beautiful fruit. It would probably taste delicious. How wonderful it would be to be as wise as God!

Eve reached up and picked some of the fruit and ate it. Then she took some to Adam, and he ate it.

After they ate the fruit, Adam and Eve noticed for the first time that they were naked. So they picked some fig leaves and sewed them together to cover themselves.

That evening they heard God walking in the garden. He was coming to visit them in the cool of the evening, as usual. But this evening Adam and Eve ran and hid behind some trees.

"Adam!" called God. "Where are you?"

Adam answered, "I heard you in the garden and I was afraid because I was naked, so I hid."

18

"Who told you that you were naked? Have you eaten the fruit that I told you not to eat?"

Adam pointed at Eve. "That woman you put here—she's the one who gave me the fruit, and I ate it."

Then God asked Eve, "Oh, Eve, how could you do such a thing?"

She answered, "It was the snake! He tricked me! That's why I did it!"

Then God said to the snake, "I'm going to punish you. From now on, you'll crawl on your belly and eat dirt. You and the woman will be enemies, and your children and her children will hate each other."

Then God said to Eve, "I'll punish you, too. You'll have to work hard at having children, and your husband will rule over you."

Then God said to Adam, "You listened to your wife and ate the fruit I told you not to eat. I'll punish the ground because of you. Thorns and thistles will grow in the fields. You'll have to work hard all your life just to get enough to eat. Then you'll die and be buried in the ground, in the soil from which I made you."

But God still cared about Adam and Eve. He gave them some new clothes that he had made for them out of animal skins. Then he told them to leave the beautiful garden.

To make sure that they would never return, he put special guards called cherubs at the entrance of the garden. These great winged creatures, like angels, held swords that turned and flashed like flames in the sunlight.

Adam and Eve never returned to their first home. Because of their disobedience, no one else ever entered the garden.

**3**

# Cain Kills His Brother

*Genesis 4*

AFTER God sent Adam and Eve from the garden of Eden, they had a hard time finding enough food to eat. Adam worked in the field all day, digging out rocks and pulling up weeds and thorns until his hands were rough and sore and his face was covered with sweat.

Eve rose early every morning to gather sticks and build the fire in front of their small hut. Then she hauled water from the stream and began her day of washing, mending, cleaning, and cooking.

Soon there were children to look after. First Adam and Eve had a son named Cain. Then they had another boy they called Abel.

How different life was now! In Eden the fruits and grains grew easily. All they had to do was reach out and pick them. In Eden they could visit with God and talk to him. In Eden they never argued or felt sad or afraid.

But even though life was more difficult, God still cared about them. They knew he was close by, watching over them.

One day Adam gathered some of the big stones he had found in the field. He put them on a pile with a wide, flat stone on top. On this altar Adam and Eve offered gifts to God and prayed to him as their Lord.

They placed their offerings on the top stone and burned them. The smoke from the burnt offerings curled upward toward heaven. Their gifts and their prayers rose together to God.

As Cain and Abel grew older, they joined their parents in the fields and at the altar. Abel became a shepherd, and Cain was a farmer.

One day Cain came to the altar with some fruit and grain he had grown. At the same time Abel brought as his offering the best part of the best lamb he had raised.

The Lord was pleased with Abel and his offering, but he wasn't pleased with Cain or his offering. Cain was upset. He clenched his teeth and frowned.

"Why are you angry?" the Lord asked Cain. "Why do you look so unhappy? If you had done the right thing, your face would show it. Watch out, Cain! Sin is crouching at your door like a wild beast, ready to pounce on you! You must overcome your anger."

But Cain ignored God's warning and didn't answer him. Instead he went to Abel and said, "Let's go out to the field."

When they got to a lonely spot where nobody could see them, Cain attacked Abel and killed him.

"Where is your brother Abel?"

Someone had seen! Cain recognized the voice of the Lord.

"How should I know? Am I my brother's keeper? Is it my job to watch over him?"

"Oh, Cain! What have you done? Listen! Your brother's blood cries out to me from the ground! This soil where you grow fruit and grain has soaked up your brother's blood! You must be punished for this murder! I won't let you farm anymore. If you try, nothing will grow for you anymore. You must leave your home and go as a stranger to other lands."

"Oh, no!" cried Cain. "I can't stand it! Don't send me away from here! Please don't send me away from you! I'll be helpless without you watching over me!"

"Don't worry. I'll take care of you."

Then the Lord put a special mark on him to show that Cain was under God's protection. Anyone who hurt Cain would be punished seven times, God told him.

Then Cain left his home, his farm, and his family. He wandered as a stranger until he came to the land of Nod, east of Eden. There Cain and his wife had children, and he built a city. Cain lived a long life and no one ever bothered him, because he was under the Lord's protection.

# Noah Builds an Ark

*Genesis 4-9*

ABEL was dead and Cain was gone. Adam and Eve were lonely without any children. So God gave them another son, whom they named Seth, to take Abel's place.

Adam and Eve lived a long time and had many more children after Seth. Seth and his brothers and sisters had children and grandchildren, and the earth began to be filled with people.

One of Seth's descendants was a man named Enoch. Enoch was famous for his good behavior and his friendship with the Lord. He pleased God so much that God took Enoch from the earth without waiting for him to die. Everyone else had to die, even those who lived for hundreds of years, like Enoch's son, Methuselah. But Enoch went to be with God while he was still alive.

As more and more people came into the world, they learned how to make and do many things. Some became herdsmen and lived in tents and took care of sheep and cattle. Others became musicians and played flutes and lyres. Some learned how to make tools from copper and iron.

But all these people forgot the Lord. They did wicked things and thought wicked thoughts.

One of Cain's descendants, Lamech, was so wicked that he bragged about killing a man who wounded him. "If anyone hurts me," said Lamech, "I'll punish him seventy-seven times!"

The Lord saw how people were living and knew what they were thinking. He felt sad.

"I'm sorry I ever made these people," he said. "Their behavior is getting worse and worse. Even their imaginations are evil. I think I'll let the earth go back to the way it was—all covered with water and dark clouds, with no living creatures on it."

But then God remembered one man who pleased him. His name was Noah.

"Noah," said God, "I've noticed how wicked everybody is. The whole world is rotten and full of crime. So I've decided to destroy everything.

"But you're different, Noah. I've seen how you

live and I know your thoughts. You're the only man in the whole world who pleases me. I'll make an agreement with you. If you do as I say, I won't destroy you and your family along with all the others.

"Here's what I want you to do," God told Noah. "Get some wood and build an ark. Make it like an enormous houseboat, four hundred and fifty feet long, seventy-five feet wide, and forty-five feet high. Put rooms in the ark, three stories of rooms, one floor above another. Put a roof on top with a window to let in the light. Put a door in the side. Then cover the ark inside and out with tar to waterproof it.

"I'm going to send a great flood to the earth," God said, "and this ark will save you from drowning. Everyone on earth will die except those inside the ark.

"You and your three sons, Shem, Ham, and Japheth, and your wife and your sons' wives will be safe in the ark. Bring animals in with you, so they'll be safe, too. I'll send you seven pairs of those that are especially useful to people and one pair of all the rest. Bring them in, male and female of each kind, so they can have families and fill the earth with their descendants after the flood.

"Don't forget to take plenty of food to store in the ark for yourself and all the others."

Noah did exactly as God said. He and his three sons cut some wood and began to build an enormous ark. They worked and worked for a long, long time because the boat was so huge. They sawed boards and hammered them together. They spread gooey black tar inside and out. Day after day, week after week, month after month, they built the ark.

Their neighbors thought Noah and his sons were ridiculous. Why would anyone make such a large ship so far from the sea? They didn't believe a flood was coming.

Finally the ark was finished. Then the Lord said to Noah, "Take your family and move in, for in seven days I will send a great flood to cover the earth. It will destroy every living creature that I have made."

Again Noah did just what the Lord commanded. He and his three sons, his wife, and his sons' wives moved into the ark. They brought the animals in after them. Then, when everyone was safely inside, the Lord closed the door behind them.

As soon as the door was shut, it began to rain. It rained so hard it seemed as though the sky had opened up. Water covered the grass and the fields, and it lifted the ark off the ground.

The rain kept coming down, and the water kept rising, higher and higher, until the ark floated away.

Still it kept raining.

The water rose up above the tops of the trees, covering the hills.

And it kept on raining.

The water rose even higher, higher than the tops of the highest mountains, so there wasn't a dry place left on the earth.

It rained for forty days and forty nights. Water covered everything. All the people and all the animals on earth drowned in the flood, everyone except Noah and his family and the animals in the ark.

Then the rain stopped.

The ark floated on the water for a long time, for weeks and months, until God sent a wind to dry up the water. Then the flood slowly began to go down, and the ark came to rest on a mountain in Ararat.

Inside the ark the people wondered whether it was safe to come out. Noah decided to open the window in the roof and send out a raven. The big black bird flew back and forth, flapping its strong wings, but it didn't return to the ark.

Then Noah sent out a little white dove. When the dove couldn't find a resting place nearby, it came right back. Noah stretched out his hand and caught it and took it inside.

A week later Noah sent the dove out again. That evening it returned with a small green olive leaf in its beak.

The people inside the ark looked at it carefully. The dove had brought them a leaf! That meant the water was going down, at least as far as the tops of the trees!

Noah waited another week, and then he sent the little dove out again. This time it didn't come back.

Was the land dry? Noah lifted off part of the roof and peeked out. He saw treetops, bushes, grass, and dry land! After living inside the ark for more than a year, everything looked beautiful to him!

It had been a strange year—first the rain and then the quiet waiting. Inside the ark it was a year without seasons, without planting time or harvest, without summer or winter, without day or night.

And now, how wonderful the dry earth looked!

"Come on out, Noah!" God was calling him. "Bring your wife and three sons and their wives and all the animals!"

Noah and his family walked out through the doorway, and right behind them came a parade of noisy creatures. Barks, neighs, roars, and screeches filled the air as the animals ran and crawled and flew from the ark.

Down the mountainside came the people and the animals.

As soon as they reached a level place, Noah gathered some stones and built an altar to give thanks to the Lord for saving him and his family from the terrible flood. He took some animals and birds and offered them as a sacrifice.

The Lord smelled the burning meat of the offering, and he was pleased.

"Never again will I punish the earth because of what people do, no matter how wicked they are," he said to himself. "Never again will I destroy all living creatures as I have just done with this flood. As long as the earth lasts, seasons will come and go. There will be planting time and harvest, summer and winter, day and night, as long as there is an earth."

Then God blessed Noah and his family.

"Go and have many children, so your descend-

ants will live all over the earth. I put you in charge of the animals, to take care of them, as well as the plants."

Then he explained, "You may kill and eat the animals. But you must never kill a person, because I've made people in my image. They're like God. Now go, have children, and scatter all over the earth."

Then God made a promise to Noah and his three sons.

"I promise you and your children after you and all the animals that came out of the ark with you, that never again will I send a flood to destroy the earth. Here's the sign of my promise: I'm putting a rainbow in the clouds. The rainbow means I'll keep my promise to you and all who live after you, now and forever."

Then Noah and his sons looked up and saw a beautiful rainbow bending across the sky. Its sparkling colors were as bright as the promises of God.

# A Tower to Reach Heaven

*Genesis 11*

**A**FTER the great flood, Noah's three sons and their wives had many children, as the Lord had commanded them. These people had children, too. Soon they were filling up the earth again, according to God's plan.

In those days there was only one language in the world. Everyone could understand everyone else.

As people moved from the east, many came to live in a valley in the land of Sumer between the Tigris and Euphrates rivers.

The people discovered that the clay soil of the valley could be shaped into bricks, and that baking them made the bricks very hard.

"Come on!" somebody suggested. "Let's make a lot of these bricks and use them to build a great city! We can live in the city and not be scattered all over the world!"

Then another person said, "Let's build an enormous tower in the middle of the city, a tower high enough to reach heaven! A tower like that will make us famous!"

The rest of the people agreed. Together they dug the clay and baked the bricks and built a great city. In the middle of the city they began to make a huge tower.

The Lord came down to look at the city and the tower that the people were building.

"Now look what they're doing!" he said to himself. "I told them to scatter to every part of the earth, but they don't want to obey me. They want to stay right where they are. They're proud of this city and the tower they're building. I know what will happen if they finish the tower. They'll think they can do anything! Well, I'm going to put a stop to it right now! I'll confuse them by mixing up their words so they won't be able to talk to each other!"

And that's exactly what he did.

You can imagine how surprised the people were when they discovered that they couldn't understand each other! Some spoke one lan-

guage; some spoke another. They spoke dozens of languages! It was very confusing.

Since they couldn't talk to each other anymore, they stopped building the tower and began to move away from the city. They left in groups of families who spoke the same language.

Some went north, some south, some east, and some west. They scattered all over the world.

Each of these groups lived as a separate people, and each spoke a different language.

The city and the tower were called Babel, which means "confusion," because the Lord confused the language of the people there. The tower was never finished, but the city stood for many years. It was known in history as Babylon.

# The Story of
# Abraham

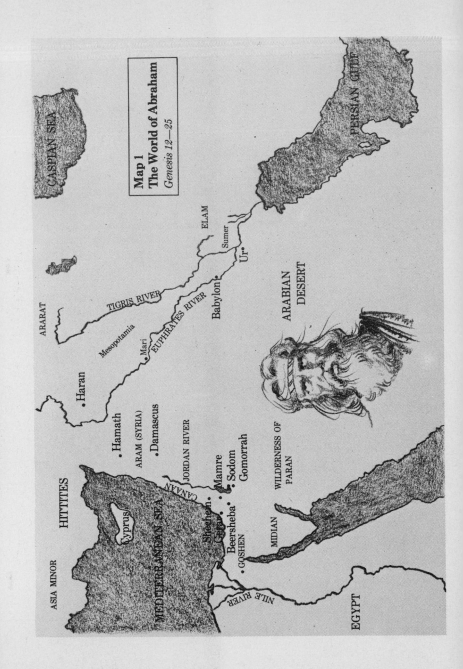

**Map 1**
**The World of Abraham**
*Genesis 12—25*

CASPIAN SEA

PERSIAN GULF

ELAM

Sumer

Ur

Babylon

ARABIAN
DESERT

TIGRIS RIVER

ARARAT

Mesopotamia

Mari

EUPHRATES RIVER

Haran

Hamath

ARAM (SYRIA)

Damascus

JORDAN RIVER

Mamre

Sodom

Gomorrah

WILDERNESS OF
PARAN

CANAAN

Shechem

Gerar

Beersheba

GOSHEN

MIDIAN

HITTITES

ASIA MINOR

Cyprus

MEDITERRANEAN SEA

NILE RIVER

EGYPT

# 6

# God Calls Abram

*Genesis 12*

AFTER the confusion at the tower, God decided to choose one family from all the scattered nations of the world. They would be his special people, and through them he would bless everyone on the earth.

The people who built the tower of Babel forgot God. They tried to become famous through their own work. God chose a man from Ur, a city near Babylon, to be the ancestor of his special people. This man became famous because of what God did through him and his family.

Ur was a busy place. Ships came to the port of Ur in the land of Sumer from Arabia and India. They brought gold, copper, ivory, lumber, and stone to trade for the rich grain of Sumer.

The Sumerians were clever people. Long before anyone else, they made wagons with wheels, they invented writing, and they made clocks and calendars. They built tools and trading ships, and they dug canals to bring river water to their fields.

But the clever Sumerian people of Ur did not worship and obey the Lord.

They bowed down to idols and worshiped the moon god of Ur in the great temple that stood in the middle of their city.

A man named Terah, a descendant of Noah's son Shem, left Ur with his family. They traveled northward, following the muddy Euphrates River. After many weeks, they came to Haran, a town six hundred miles northwest of Ur.

Terah died in Haran. One day his son Abram told his family to get ready to move again. God had talked to him.

The Lord had said to Abram, "Go from your native land and your father's house to a land that I will show you. If you follow me, I'll give you many descendants, and they'll become a great nation. I'll bless you and make you famous. All the peoples of the earth will receive my blessing through you."

What did it mean? Where was the Lord leading

him? Would there be trouble or danger on the way?

Abram did not know what lay ahead, but he wanted to obey God. His wife, Sarai, and his nephew Lot agreed to go with him. Lot was the son of Abram's youngest brother, Haran, who had died at Ur. None of them knew anything about the land where they were going.

They packed everything they owned in bundles and put them on the backs of their donkeys. Clay pots, goatskin bottles, straw mats, goat hair tents—all of Abram's possessions, along with the donkeys, sheep, and goats, and his servants—everything was ready to go.

Sarai hugged the children, not their own children, for Abram and Sarai had no children of their own, but Nahor's children. They were leaving Abram's brother Nahor and his family behind in Haran.

They said good-bye one last time and headed south, toward the land of Canaan.

They moved slowly. Every once in a while they stopped to rest under the shade of the fig and olive trees. While the animals grazed on the grasslands and drank water from the cool mountain streams, the people filled their goatskin bottles and baked a simple bread on a campfire.

They traveled past vineyards and wheat fields, past the cities of Halab, Hamath, and Damascus, on and on for about a month. Finally they reached the land of Canaan.

Abram followed the Lord to the hill country of Canaan. He came to an old oak tree at Shechem, and there he stopped.

The Lord appeared to Abram and said, "This is the country that I'm going to give to you and your descendants."

Abram built an altar there to honor the Lord. Then he moved on, to a place in the hills, where he set up his tents and made another altar and worshiped the Lord.

# 7

# Abram and Lot Choose Land

*Genesis 12-13*

FOR the rest of his life Abram lived in tents, out in the fields away from the towns of the Canaanites who already lived in the land. He moved with the seasons, going south in the summer and north in the winter, always looking for water and pasture for his animals. The people in the towns looked down on Abram and other people who wandered from place to place, because they looked rough and owned no land.

That first year in Canaan there was a famine.

There wasn't enough food for the people or animals. Abram decided to take his family to the land of Egypt to find food.

As they came near the border of Egypt, he began to worry.

"Sarai," he said, "these Egyptians are rich and powerful. You're such a beautiful woman the Egyptians will notice you. They'll want to take you away from me. If they think I'm your husband, they'll kill me. Tell them you're my sister, and then they won't kill me. If they think I'm your brother they will let me live and treat me well."

When they arrived in Egypt, some of the men from the palace noticed Sarai and went to tell Pharaoh about her. The Egyptian king already had many wives, but he wanted to marry Sarai.

Things happened then as Abram had expected. Pharaoh's men took Sarai to the palace and they gave Abram flocks of sheep and goats, cattle, donkeys, camels, and slaves.

But the Lord didn't like what was going on. He sent terrible sickness to Pharaoh and the others in the palace.

Pharaoh recognized the power of Abram's God, and he sent for Abram at once.

"What have you done to me?" he demanded. "Why didn't you tell me Sarai was your wife? and let me take her for my wife? Well, here's your wife! Take her and get out!"

Then he ordered his guards to take Abram and

all his possessions and put him out of the country.

Abram and Lot and their servants headed north, back to the hill country of Canaan. He was traveling slower now, for he owned many more animals, and it took longer for them to eat and drink. He had become a rich man with gold and silver as well as animals and slaves from Egypt.

Finally they reached the spot in the hills where they had camped earlier. Abram went back to the place where he had built an altar and worshiped the Lord. As he finished praying, he heard the sound of angry voices.

Trouble was breaking out in the camp. The men in charge of Abram's cattle were fighting with Lot's men. Abram's nephew, Lot, had become a rich man, too, with flocks and herds and tents of his own. With so many animals, there never seemed to be enough grazing land.

This rocky hill country was all right for sheep and goats, but the cattle didn't have enough pasture. Things were getting nasty.

"Let's stop quarreling," Abram said to Lot. "We've been arguing ever since we left Egypt. It's not good for us or our cattlemen to fight. After all, Lot, we're members of the same family! There's enough land around here for both of us.

"I have an idea. Let's break up into two groups. You pick whatever part of the land you want, and I'll take what's left. You and your family go one way, and I'll go the other."

Lot looked around. From where he stood high in the hills he could see the dry, rocky land of Canaan to the west and the rich, green valley of the Jordan River to the east. The river valley was green with trees and bushes. It looked as fertile as the land of Egypt. The garden of Eden couldn't have been more beautiful.

Lot chose the Jordan valley.

Abram agreed, and so they parted.

Abram stayed in the west, in the land of

Canaan, and Lot went east, down to the valley of the Jordan. He followed the valley south, to the cities of the plain. There he pitched his tents, settling near Sodom. The people of Sodom were great sinners and did not please the Lord, but later Lot and his family moved into the city.

After Lot left, the Lord spoke to Abram.

"Look all around you. All this land, as far as you can see in every direction, will be yours forever. I'm going to give it to you and your descendants. And I'm going to give you so many descendants that nobody will be able to count them! They'll be like the dust of the earth!

"Walk from one end of the land to the other, for I'm giving it all to you!"

Abram looked all around at the hills and valleys, the fields and towns of the land of Canaan, sparkling green and gold in the sunlight. All this God promised would belong to Abram and his descendants!

Then Abram pitched his tents in a grove of oak trees, at a place called Mamre, in the hill country. As soon as he was settled, he built an altar and worshiped God.

# Abram's Adventure with the Kings and His Covenant with God

*Genesis 14—15*

**W**HILE Abram was living in his tent in the hill country, and Lot was living in his house in Sodom, a war broke out.

All five cities were ruled by kings. These kings were ruled by a more important king from Elam, and he was angry because the five kings no longer obeyed him.

The five kings got their men together and

fought a battle against the invaders from the east. They were defeated, and many of their men were killed. The valley where the battle was fought was full of tar pits. As they ran away from the battle, some of the men from Sodom and Gomorrah fell into the sticky pits. Others escaped to the hills.

While the men were stuck in the tar pits, the army from the east went into Sodom and Gomorrah and took everything they could carry away. They even took the people to be their slaves. Poor Lot and his family were captured with everyone else from Sodom.

The army marched away with the loot and the people, but one of the prisoners escaped and ran to tell Abram what had happened.

Abram quickly called together all the young men in his camp—servants, slaves, shepherds, and cattlemen. Altogether there were 318 men who had been born in his household. Abram led them after the army of the enemy.

They followed the army up the Jordan valley, all the way north of Damascus to the place where the river begins.

That night, Abram's men surprised the enemy with a sneak attack in the dark. The enemy soldiers were so confused that they ran away, leaving behind the people and the loot from Sodom and Gomorrah. How happy Lot and the other prisoners were to see their rescuers!

Meanwhile, the kings of Sodom and Gomorrah

returned home to their empty cities. When the king of Sodom heard about how Abram and his men had rescued everything, he came out to meet him. With him came Melchizedek, the king of Salem.

Melchizedek was also a priest of God the Most High. He brought Abram bread and wine and blessed him.

"Blessed be Abram by God Most High, who made heaven and earth! And praises to God Most High, who has given you victory over your enemies!" he said.

Abram gave Melchizedek a tenth of everything he had rescued from the army of the enemy

Then the king of Sodom said to Abram, "Keep the rest of the loot for yourself. I just want my people back!"

"No," said Abram. "I don't want anything for myself. I promised the Lord Most High, who made heaven and earth, that I wouldn't take anything from you. Just let my friends have their share."

Then Abram returned to his tent, and Lot went back to Sodom.

Soon after his adventure with the kings, Abram had a vision. During the vision he heard the voice of the Lord.

"Don't be afraid, Abram. I am your shield," God said. "I'll protect you and give you a great reward."

"O Lord God, what good are your gifts when I

still have no children?" Abram replied. "You haven't given me a son to inherit my property, so one of my servants will get everything when I die."

"No, your servant won't be your heir. A child of your own will inherit your property," God promised.

He took Abram outside.

"Look up into the sky, Abram, and count the stars—if you can! That's how many descendants you'll have!"

Abram was growing old and he and Sarai still had no children of their own, but he trusted the Lord and believed the promise. Because of Abram's great faith, the Lord was pleased with him.

A few days later, the Lord spoke to Abram again.

"I am the Lord, who brought you out of Ur to give you this land for your own."

Abram replied, "O Lord God, how can I be sure that it will be mine?"

"I'll make a covenant with you," the Lord told Abram. "Bring me a calf, a goat, and a ram for a sacrifice, and bring along a dove and a young pigeon."

Abram understood that a covenant was a serious agreement, like a contract. Sacrificing animals while making a covenant was like signing a contract, or swearing to a promise.

He brought the animals and cut them in half and arranged the pieces in two rows. Birds of prey swooped down on the pieces, but Abram drove them off.

That evening, just as the sun was setting, Abram fell into a deep sleep. A dark and dreadful feeling came over him.

Then the Lord said, "I want you to know that your descendants will be strangers in a foreign land. They'll be slaves there, and their masters will treat them cruelly for four hundred years. But I'll punish the nation that oppresses them.

At last they will escape, taking great wealth with them. As for you, you'll live to a happy old age and die and be buried in peace."

Then the sun went down, and it was very dark.

Out of the darkness appeared a smoking pot of fire and a flaming torch. They passed mysteriously between the two rows of the offering.

Then the Lord spoke.

"All this land, from the border of Egypt all the way to the Euphrates, and all the lands between, I give to your descendants."

God had signed the contract, and had made an important agreement with Abram. He had promised to give Abram many descendants and much land. For his part, Abram promised to obey the Lord. God would keep his promise as long as Abram and his family were faithful.

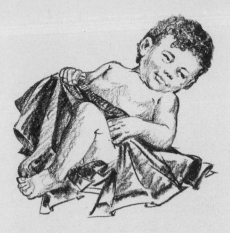

# God Changes Abram's Name

*Genesis 16—17*

A BRAM and Sarai lived in Canaan for ten
years and still had no children.

One day Sarai said to her husband,
"I'm getting old, and I don't have any children of
my own. I'm tired of waiting for a son! Why don't
you take my Egyptian slave girl, Hagar, and
treat her like a second wife? According to the old
custom, if you have a child by her, it will count as
mine."

Abram agreed to go along with Sarai's sugges-
tion, and he took Hagar as his wife. After a while

Hagar discovered that she was going to have a baby. This made her feel important, and she was rude to Sarai.

"It's not fair!" Sarai complained to Abram. "Just because Hagar's expecting a baby, she thinks she's better than I am! She looks down on me, and it's all your fault! I know it was my idea to give her to you, but look what happened! I won't put up with it!"

"All right, Sarai. Take her back. She can be your servant again. You're in charge of her. Do whatever you want."

Then Sarai took Hagar back to be her servant again. But she was angry with Hagar and treated her unkindly. She was so mean that Hagar ran away.

She went out into the desert, along the road to Egypt, her native land. When she came to a well, she stopped to rest and have a drink of water.

There beside the well an angel of the Lord found her.

"Hagar, slave of Sarai," the angel said, "where are you coming from, and where are you going?"

"I'm running away from my mistress, Sarai."

"God has heard you, Hagar. He sees you and knows your problems," the angel told her. "If you obey God, he'll help you. Go back to Sarai and be polite and kind to her. Do what she tells you. You're going to have a son. Call him Ishmael, which means 'God Hears,' because the Lord has heard you. When your son grows up, he'll live in the wilderness, as wild and free as an untamed colt. Through him you'll have many descendants—so many that no one will be able to count them."

Hagar realized that the Lord himself was speaking to her through the angel.

"I've actually seen God, and I'm alive to tell about it!" she said to herself. She called that place Beer Lahai Roi, which means "Well of the Living One Who Sees Me."

Then she returned to Sarai and worked for her, as the Lord had told her. A few months later she had a baby boy, and he was named Ishmael.

Thirteen years passed. Hagar stayed in Abram's camp, working as Sarai's servant, and Ishmael grew up in the tents of his father.

One day the Lord appeared to Abram and said, "I am God the Almighty. If you follow my ways and do what's right, I'll keep my covenant with you."

Abram bowed down before the Lord.

The Lord said to him, "I'll give you many descendants. You'll be the father of many nations. From now on your name isn't Abram, but Abraham, which means 'father of many.' I'm giving all this land of Canaan to you and your children and your children's children forever. If you follow my ways and do what's right, I'll keep my promises to you and to them forever. And I'll be their God."

Then the Lord said to him, "As for you, Abram, here's a sign that you and your family are keeping my covenant. All your men and boys must be dedicated to me. Circumcision will be the sign of our agreement. Dedicate all the boy babies when they are eight days old.

"I'm giving Sarai a new name, too," God told Abraham. "From now on her name will be Sarah, which means 'princess.' I'll bless her and give you a son by her. She'll be the mother of many nations, and you and Sarah will be the ancestors of kings!"

Abraham laughed to himself. "An old man like me a father? How can it be? Sarah will have a child? She's too old a woman for that!"

Then he said out loud, "Yes, bless my son Ishmael!"

"No," said God. "I don't mean your son Ishmael. I mean another son, the son of Sarah. Call him Isaac, which means 'Laughter.' I'll keep my promises with Isaac and his descendants forever.

"As for Ishmael, I know you love him very much. I'll certainly bless him, too," God said. "I'll give him many descendants also. He'll be the ancestor of twelve princes, and I'll make a great nation of his descendants.

"But my special covenant will be with Isaac, who will be born to Sarah this time next year."

As soon as he finished speaking to Abraham, God left him.

Then Abraham took his son Ishmael and all his servants and circumcised them as a sign of their agreement with God. Abraham also was circumcised to remind him of his covenant with the Lord.

# Abraham's Mysterious Visitors

*Genesis 18—19*

ONE hot afternoon Abraham was sitting in the shade at the entrance of his tent. He looked up and saw three men coming toward him. There was something unusual about them, but he didn't notice it at first.

Abraham ran out to meet the strangers. Wanting to treat the men as honored guests, Abraham offered to feed them.

He bowed low and said, "Sirs, don't pass by my home without stopping! Let me serve you. I'll send for some water so you can wash the dust off your feet. Rest here beneath the shady oaks while I bring you some bread. It will give you strength for the journey that has brought you my way. You've honored me by coming here, so let me take good care of you."

"Very well," answered the visitors. "Go ahead."

Abraham hurried into the tent and called to Sarah.

"Quick! Get a sack of the best flour! Make some buns!"

Then he ran and picked out one of his best calves. He took the animal to a servant, who quickly prepared the veal and cooked it. Then he took some milk and yogurt along with the meat and set the food out in front of the visitors.

Abraham stood near the three men under the trees while they ate.

"Where is your wife, Sarah?" they asked him.

"In there, in the tent," Abraham answered.

Then one of the visitors said, "When I return next year, your wife Sarah will have a son!"

Sarah was listening at the entrance of the tent. She laughed to herself.

"Abraham and I are both much too old to have babies! How could I have a child?"

Then the same man spoke to Abraham again. "Why did Sarah laugh and say she's too old to have a child? Is anything too hard for the Lord? Remember, I'll be back this time next year, and Sarah will have a son!"

Suddenly Sarah felt afraid. "I didn't laugh!" she lied.

"Yes, you did," he said.

Then the three men got up to go. Abraham walked along with them to the top of a hill. From there they could look down at the cities of the plain. Two of the men turned toward the road that led down to Sodom. But the man who had spoken to Sarah stopped to talk to Abraham.

He thought to himself before he spoke. "Shall I hide from Abraham what I'm going to do? Abraham will be the father of a great nation. All the nations on earth will be blessed through him. I've chosen him to teach his family to keep the way of the Lord by doing what's right and good. If Abraham's descendants obey me, I'll keep my promises."

Then he said to Abraham, "I've heard about the sinners of Sodom and Gomorrah. Shameful things are told about them. I must go down and find out if these stories are true."

The other two continued on their way to Sodom, but the third man still stood in front of Abraham.

By now Abraham had guessed who his mysterious visitors were: the Lord and his angels appearing in human form. Abraham also guessed that the Lord planned to destroy Sodom.

"Are you going to punish the good people along with the bad?" Abraham asked the Lord. "What if there are fifty innocent people in the city? Will you destroy it, and not pardon the city for the sake of the good people inside? Surely you wouldn't kill the good people along with the bad ones? You wouldn't do that! Doesn't the Judge of all the world do what's right?"

"If I find fifty good people in Sodom, I'll pardon the whole city for their sake," the Lord told Abraham.

"Please forgive me for being so bold, Lord. I'm

only a man. But suppose there are five fewer than fifty? Will you destroy the whole city because of them?"

"No, I won't destroy it if I find forty-five good people there."

"What if you find only forty?"

"I won't destroy it for the sake of the forty."

"Please don't be impatient, Lord, but what if you find only thirty?"

"I won't destroy it if I find thirty."

"Please forgive my boldness again, Lord. Suppose there are only twenty?"

"I won't destroy it for the sake of the twenty."

"Don't be angry, Lord, if I speak just once more. What if there are only ten?"

"I won't destroy Sodom if I find ten innocent people in the city."

When the Lord finished speaking with Abraham, he left, and Abraham returned home.

Meanwhile, the other two mysterious visitors were nearing Sodom. When they arrived that evening, the angels found Abraham's nephew, Lot, sitting at the city gate. They looked for ten innocent people, but Lot was the only good man they could find in the whole city.

When Lot saw the strangers, he got up and went to greet them. He bowed low with his face to the ground.

"Please, sirs," he said, as friendly as Abraham had been earlier. "Come to my home and spend the night. You can wash your feet there and rest.

Then in the morning you can get up early and be on your way."

"No," they answered, "we'll spend the night here in the city square."

But Lot insisted, and finally they went along with him to his house. He baked some flat bread and fixed a nice meal for them. When the food was ready, they ate.

Before they went to bed that night, they heard loud voices outside the house. It sounded like a riot.

All the men of Sodom had come to Lot's house. They had surrounded the building and they were calling out to him.

"Where are those men who came here tonight? Bring them out to us so we can attack them!"

Lot met them outside at the entrance and closed the front door behind him.

"Please, my friends, don't be so wicked," said Lot. "Look, I have two unmarried daughters. Let me bring them out to you. Do anything you want to them. But don't attack these men. They're my guests. Please, they're under my protection."

"Get out of our way!" the Sodomites answered. "Who do you think you are, anyway? You foreigner! What makes you think you can tell us how to behave? Watch out, Lot! We'll treat you worse than we're going to treat them!"

They began to push and shove Lot. They moved forward to break down the door.

Just then the mysterious strangers reached out

their hands and pulled Lot back into the house and shut the door.

Then they struck the men of Sodom with a blinding light, so they couldn't see. The Sodomites fumbled around, bumping into each other, unable to find the way into Lot's house.

Then the angels said to Lot, "Do you have any relatives in this city? If you do, get them out of ͟ere right away. We're going to destroy this place! The Lord has heard about the wickedness of the people, and he has sent us to destroy the city!"

Lot went out to find the men who were planning to marry his daughters.

"Hurry and get out of here," he told them, "for the Lord is going to destroy the city!"

But they just looked at him as if he were joking.

By the time he got back, the night was nearly over and the sun was about to rise.

"Quick! Get your wife and your two daughters!" the angels said. "Hurry up or you'll all be killed when the city is punished!"

But Lot hesitated. Then the Lord had pity on him, and the angels took Lot and his wife and his daughters by the hand and led them out of Sodom.

When they were outside the city, the angels said, "Run for your lives! Don't look back or stop anywhere in the plain. Run to the hills, or you'll be killed."

"Oh, no, sirs!" begged Lot. "You've done me a great favor and saved my life, but the hills are so far away! I can't get there in time! See that little town over there? It's near enough for us to reach quickly. Let us go there—it's very small—and we'll be safe."

The Lord answered Lot through the angels. "All right, do as you wish. I won't destroy that town. But hurry. Run fast! I can't do anything until you get there!"

The sun had come up by the time Lot reached the safety of the little town of Zoar.

Then the Lord rained down fire and brimstone upon Sodom and Gomorrah. The earth shook and burning tar pits spit flames high into the air. The Lord destroyed those cities and all the plain, along with everyone who lived there and everything that grew on the land. Burning tar covered the cities.

But Lot's wife looked back, and she turned into a pillar of salt. She had disobeyed the Lord.

Lot was so frightened that he soon left Zoar. He and his daughters moved up into the hills and hid themselves in a cave.

The morning when God destroyed Sodom Abraham got up early. He went to the hilltop where he had talked to the Lord the day before. He looked down at the plain. Thick smoke rose from the earth like fumes from a giant furnace. Sodom and Gomorrah had disappeared.

# A Boy Named Laughter

*Genesis 20—21*

SOON after the destruction of Sodom and Gomorrah, Abraham moved his tents from Mamre to Gerar, in the desert of southwestern Canaan. He found pasture there for his animals and lived at peace with his neighbors. The people of Gerar saw that Abraham was a prophet, and that God was with him in everything he did.

About a year later, just as the Lord had promised, Sarah had a son. Abraham named the baby Isaac, meaning "Laughter."

"God has brought me joy and laughter!" said Sarah. "Everybody who hears about it will laugh with me! Who would have thought that Abraham and I could have a baby? Yet, here he is—a son for Abraham in his old age!"

When Isaac was about two years old, Abraham gave a great feast for him. During the party Sarah noticed that Hagar's son was teasing her son Isaac.

She complained to Abraham. "Get rid of that slave and her son! I won't have that woman's son living here with us one more day! No son of hers is going to share Isaac's inheritance!"

This upset Abraham, for Ishmael was his son, too.

"Don't worry about the boy or his mother," God told Abraham. "Do whatever Sarah says. Isaac is your special son. He will receive all that you own when you die. Through him you'll have the descendants that I've promised. As for Ishmael, I'll make his descendants a great nation, too, because he's your child also."

The next morning Abraham got up early and took some bread and a goatskin of water to Hagar and Ishmael. He put them on her back and sent her away into the desert.

Hagar left the camp, as she had done fifteen years before, when she had run away from Sarah. However, this time she missed the road and became lost in the desert of Beersheba.

She wandered aimlessly in the heat of the

desert. Their water was soon gone. Ishmael was hot and thirsty, but Hagar had nothing to give him. She left him crying under a bush and walked away.

When she was a little distance from him, she sat down and said to herself, "He's going to die of thirst and I can't stand to watch him suffer."

Then she began to cry, too.

God heard them crying. Then an angel of God called to Hagar from heaven, "What's the matter, Hagar? Don't be afraid. God has heard you.

He knows your problem. Get up and take care of your boy. I'm going to make a great nation of his descendants."

Then God opened her eyes and she saw a spring of water right there in the middle of the desert. She filled the goatskin and gave Ishmael a drink.

God stayed with Ishmael as he grew up. Living in the desert, the boy became an expert hunter with a bow and arrow. He settled in the wilderness of Paran and married a wife his mother found for him in Egypt.

# God Tests Abraham

*Genesis 22*

A BRAHAM moved from Gerar to Beersheba, on the edge of the desert, where he lived many years.

Isaac, the beloved son of his old age, grew up in Beersheba. He was becoming a strong and healthy boy.

One day God decided to test Abraham. "Abraham!" he called.

"Yes, Lord. Here I am!"

"Take your son, your dear son Isaac, and go to the land of Moriah. There on a hill that I'll show you, sacrifice him to me as a burnt offering."

A burnt offering? Abraham knew that human sacrifice, even child sacrifice, was common among the Canaanites. But surely the Lord didn't want a human sacrifice like his neighbors offered to their gods! And what about the promises for Isaac's future?

But Abraham had promised always to obey God. Early the next morning he got up, split some firewood, and saddled his donkey. He took two of his servants and Isaac and set out for the land of Moriah.

They walked north from Beersheba for three days, stopping at night to rest.

On the third day Abraham saw the hill of Moriah in the distance. He turned to the servants. "You stay down here with the donkey while the boy and I go up there to worship. We'll be back."

Then he unloaded the wood from the donkey's back and laid it across Isaac's shoulders. He unpacked the flint for making fire, and a sharp knife, and carried them himself.

The two of them walked on together.

After a while Isaac spoke up. "Father?"

"Yes, my son."

"I see you've got the flint and the wood, but where is the lamb for the burnt offering?"

"God himself will provide the lamb, my son."

And they walked on together.

At last they came to the place on top of the hill

that God had told him about.

Abraham built an altar. He arranged the wood on top. He tied Isaac's hands and feet. He laid the boy on the altar on top of the wood.

Then he put out his hand to pick up the knife to kill his son.

Just then the angel of the Lord called to him from heaven. "Abraham! Abraham!"

"Yes, here I am!"

"Don't touch the boy! Don't do a thing to him!

Now I know that you're faithful and obedient. You haven't even kept your own dear son from me."

Then Abraham looked around and saw a ram caught in a thicket by its horns. He went over and took the ram and laid it on the altar as a burnt offering, instead of his son.

Then the angel of the Lord called to Abraham again from heaven. "This is the word of the Lord. Because you didn't keep your dear son from me, I'll richly bless you and give you many descendants. You'll have as many descendants as there are stars in the sky or grains of sand along the seashore. They'll conquer all their enemies. And all the nations of the earth will ask me to bless them as I have blessed your descendants. All this will happen because you have obeyed my command!' "

Abraham called that place by a Hebrew name which means, "God Provides."

Then he went back down the hill. He and Isaac and the servants returned together to Beersheba.

# 13

# Finding a Wife for Isaac

*Genesis 22—25*

**A**BRAHAM and Sarah were pleased with Isaac, the son of their old age. They were glad to hear that Abraham's family back in Haran was growing, too. They received news that Abraham's brother, Nahor, was now the father of twelve grown sons and had many grandchildren.

Sarah lived many more years. When she died Abraham mourned and cried for her. He realized that he had no place to bury his wife, so he went to see the leaders of a nearby town.

"I'm a foreigner here," he began. "I am not allowed to own property in your country. But my wife has just died, and I have no place to bury her. Would you let me buy just enough land for a decent burial place?"

"Sir," they answered, "we respect you as a mighty prince. Bury your wife in one of our best graves. We would be honored."

"No, that won't do. If you're willing to let me bury my wife in your country, sell me a piece of property. I'll pay whatever you ask."

Finally they agreed and named their price. Abraham weighed out four hundred pieces of silver for a field which contained a burial cave. This land in Machpelah, east of Mamre, was the only land Abraham ever owned in Canaan.

He buried Sarah in the cave in the field.

Abraham was now an old, old man. Before he died, he made one last request. He called in his chief servant, the man who was in charge of all his property.

"I want you to solemnly promise by the Lord, the God of heaven and earth, that you won't get a wife for my son from the women of Canaan," Abraham said. "You must go at once to Haran, to the country where my brother's family still lives, and find a wife for Isaac there."

"But, sir, what if I find a woman to be his wife and she isn't willing to come back here to Canaan with me?" the servant asked. "Do you want me to take your son back there if that happens?"

"No!" said Abraham. "Never take my son back there! Not for any reason! The Lord God of heaven took me from my father's house and from the land of my relatives, and he promised that he would give this land to my descendants. He'll send his angel on ahead of you, and you'll find a wife for my son. But whatever happens, don't take my son there!"

The servant solemnly promised to do what Abraham asked.

He took ten of Abraham's camels and some of the other servants and set out for Haran. He took with him all kinds of gifts from his master.

After a long journey, they came near the city. It was almost evening as they stopped beside a well outside Haran.

The well was a large, deep hole with steps leading down to a spring. Above was a watering trough for the animals.

Abraham's servant made the tired and thirsty camels kneel down next to the well. He noticed that it was the time of day when the women of the city came out to get water.

"O Lord, God of my master Abraham," the servant prayed, "help me! The women of the city are on their way here to draw water. Which one have you chosen for Isaac? Show me. I'll ask one of them for a drink. If she's the one, let her give me some water and then offer water for the camels also."

Just as he finished praying, a beautiful young

woman came to the well with a water jug on her shoulder. It was Rebecca, the granddaughter of Abraham's brother Nahor.

Rebecca went down to the well and filled her jar. As she came up again, the servant hurried over to her and said, "Please, may I have a sip of water?"

"Drink, sir," she answered, quickly lowering the jar to pour him a drink.

When he finished, she said, "Now let me draw some water for your camels, also."

She quickly emptied her jar into the water trough and hurried back to the well to get more water.

He watched her quietly, waiting to find out whether this was the one the Lord had chosen for Isaac.

She drew enough water for all the camels!

He took out a gold ring and two gold bracelets and gave them to her.

"Whose daughter are you?" he asked. "Tell me, please."

"I'm Rebecca, the daughter of Bethuel and Milcah, and granddaughter of Nahor."

"Is there room in your father's house for us to spend the night?" the servant asked.

"We have plenty of straw and feed for the camels and lots of room for you," she answered.

The servant bowed his head and worshiped. "Blessed be the Lord, the God of my master Abraham! How faithful and kind he is! He has led me

straight to the house of my master's relatives!"

Then Rebecca ran off to her mother's house to tell everyone what had happened. Her brother Laban was excited when he heard the news and saw the ring and bracelets. He went out to the well and found the man still standing beside the camels.

"Come," Laban said. "Everything is ready for you! Come to our house, and bring your men and the camels with you!"

They went together to the house. Laban unloaded the camels and gave them straw and feed. He brought water to the visitors so they could wash their feet.

But when food was set out for him, Abraham's servant said, "I won't eat until I've told my story."

"Let's hear it!" they all said.

"I'm the servant of Abraham," he began. "The Lord has greatly blessed my master, and he has become a wealthy man. He owns many sheep, cattle, camels, and donkeys, much silver and gold, and many servants. My master's wife, Sarah, gave him a son in his old age, and Abraham is leaving everything he owns to this son, Isaac.

"My master made me solemnly promise to find a wife for Isaac here among his relatives in Haran. He told me the angel of the Lord would guide me to the woman the Lord has chosen."

Then he told them what had happened that

evening at the well. "Now, then," he finished, "tell me what you think of my story. What do you say?"

"This is indeed the Lord's doing," Laban answered. "It's not for us to say. Here's Rebecca. Take her back to marry your master's son, according to the will of the Lord."

As soon as the servant heard this, he bowed down and worshiped the Lord. Then he brought out gifts of gold and silver and clothing, and he handed them to Rebecca. He gave expensive presents to her mother and brother, too. Then he and his men ate and drank and went to bed.

In the morning Abraham's servant said, "I'm ready to leave now. Let me return to my master at once."

"Oh, no," Rebecca's mother and brother protested. "Let her stay with us a few more days, just a week or maybe ten days."

"Don't delay me," Abraham's servant said. "The Lord has guided me and now I must return to my master."

They called in Rebecca.

"Are you willing to go back to Canaan with this man?" they asked.

"Yes," she answered, "I am."

So they said good-bye to Rebecca and Abraham's servant and his men. They kissed her and gave her a wedding blessing as she left. Then Rebecca and her maids got up on their camels and followed Abraham's men back to Canaan.

Isaac was waiting near Beersheba, where he lived. One evening he went out to the fields for a walk. He looked up and saw camels approaching from the north.

Seated on one of the camels, Rebecca was looking at this strange new land. She was the first person in the caravan to spot Isaac.

"Who's that man out there in the field walking toward us?" she asked.

"That's my master, Isaac," the servant answered.

She quickly covered herself with her veil.

When the caravan reached Isaac, the servant told him everything that had happened on the journey.

Then Isaac took Rebecca into his tent, and she became his wife. Isaac loved Rebecca and they lived together happily for many years.

Abraham lived to a happy old age and died and was buried in peace. His sons, Isaac and Ishmael, buried him in the cave of Machpelah, next to Sarah.

Ishmael lived in the wilderness and had twelve sons. They were the ancestors of twelve tribes who lived in the Arabian desert.

Abraham left everything he owned to his son Isaac. And God blessed Isaac.

# The Story of
# Jacob

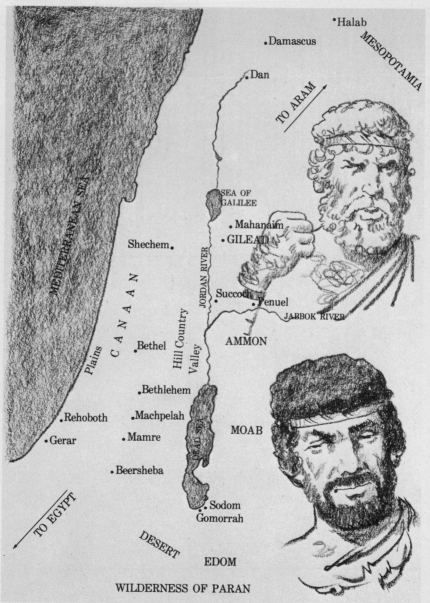

# Map 2
# The World of Isaac and Jacob
*Genesis 25—35*

MEDITERRANEAN SEA

Halab

Damascus

MESOPOTAMIA

Dan

TO ARAM

SEA OF GALILEE

Mahanaim

GILEAD

Shechem

JORDAN RIVER

C A N A A N

Succoth

Penuel

JABBOK RIVER

Plains

Bethel

Hill Country

Valley

AMMON

Bethlehem

Rehoboth

Machpelah

DEAD SEA

MOAB

Gerar

Mamre

Beersheba

TO EGYPT

Sodom

Gomorrah

DESERT

EDOM

WILDERNESS OF PARAN

# 14

# The Fighting Twins and Their Peaceful Father

*Genesis 25—26*

FOR many years Isaac and Rebecca lived in their tents at Beersheba. Isaac had received all of Abraham's property. Isaac and his wife had everything they could wish for—everything that is, except what they wanted most. They had no children.

Isaac remembered how his mother Sarah had to wait many years for a child of her own. Perhaps the Lord would give Rebecca children after all. He prayed about it, and the Lord answered his prayer. They were going to be parents!

But something was wrong.

As the time for the birth grew near, Rebecca began to feel very uncomfortable. What was that terrible pain? She didn't know it, but she was carrying twins, and they were struggling inside her!

"I feel awful!" she cried, and she went to ask the Lord about it.

"You're going to have twins," he told her. "They'll be the ancestors of two enemy nations. That's why the babies are struggling inside you. One will be stronger than the other, and the older baby will be the servant of the younger one."

So she had twins.

The first-born was all covered with thick red hair, so they named him Esau, meaning "hairy."

The second baby was born holding on tightly to the heel of his brother. He was called Jacob, which means "Heel Grabber" or "Sneaky."

How different the two brothers were!

As they grew up, their behavior was even more different than their appearance. Esau was rough and loud. He loved to go hunting in the fields, and he became an expert with a bow and arrow. Jacob was a quiet person who enjoyed staying at home.

Isaac preferred Esau. He enjoyed eating the wild game that the hairy twin brought back from his hunting. But Rebecca preferred Jacob.

Jacob and his mother were sorry that Esau was the older son. According to the law, the first-born would receive twice as much property as the other children, and he would become the head of the family when the father died.

One day when Jacob was cooking some red lentils, his brother Esau came in from the fields. Esau was tired and hungry. When he smelled the food, he said, "Give me some of that red stew! I'm starving!"

"First give me your right as the first-born son," answered Jacob.

"All right, all right," said Esau. "Here I am, practically starving to death, and you want to talk about the birthright! What good is that to me?" And he reached for the food.

"Wait a minute!" said Jacob, stopping him. "First you must give me your solemn promise!"

So Esau made a vow and gave up his birthright to Jacob.

Then Jacob gave him some bread and the red lentil stew.

Esau ate and drank, got up, and left. That's how little he cared about his birthright.

Some time after this there was a famine in Canaan. The people did not have enough food or water. Isaac decided to take his family to Egypt, as his father Abraham had done many years before.

But the Lord came to Isaac and said, "Don't go to Egypt. Stay here in Canaan. I'll show you a place where you can find food and water. If you obey me, I'll stay with you and bless you. I'll keep my promise to your father Abraham through you. I'll give all this land to you and your descendants. You'll have as many descendants as there are stars in the sky, and I'll give this whole country to them. All the nations of the earth will receive my blessing through you. All this will happen because your father Abraham obeyed me and did what was right."

Isaac listened to the Lord and went to Gerar.

He planted a crop there, and later that year he had an enormous harvest. The Lord blessed Isaac. He grew richer and richer until he was a wealthy man. He had so many sheep and cattle, oxen and donkeys, servants, and other property that the people of Gerar became jealous.

Some of them went out and found all the wells that Abraham's servants had dug many years earlier, when Abraham lived in Gerar. They filled the wells with dirt so Isaac couldn't use them.

Isaac cleaned up the wells so they could be used again. Then the people of Gerar complained to Abimelech, their king. Abimelech went to see Isaac.

"Go away!" Abimelech told Isaac. "We don't want you here any more. We don't like you foreigners coming here and getting rich in our land! Get out of here!"

So Isaac moved away from Gerar. He pitched his tents in a dry valley in the desert nearby.

He sent his servants out to dig a well in the valley. Soon they found a spring of running water, but before they could water their animals, the shepherds of Gerar came and picked a fight with Isaac's servants. "This water belongs to us!" they shouted.

Isaac told his men to move on and look for water somewhere else.

They dug another well, but the shepherds of Gerar returned and made trouble over that one, too.

Isaac told his men to move on again.

They dug another well, and this time the shepherds of Gerar left them alone.

"We'll be all right," said Isaac. "The Lord has

given us plenty of room." He named that place Rehoboth, meaning "plenty of room."

After a while he and his family returned to Beersheba. The night he arrived, the Lord appeared to him. "I am the God of your father Abraham," he said. "Don't be afraid, for I am with you. I'll bless you and give you many descendants for the sake of my servant Abraham." Isaac built an altar there and prayed to the Lord.

A little while later Abimelech came from Gerar with his chief adviser and the commander of his army.

"Why have you come all the way out here to see me?" Isaac asked.

"We want to be friends," Abimelech answered.

"You weren't very friendly the last time we met," Isaac pointed out.

"That's true," said Abimelech, "but we've seen that the Lord is with you. He blessed you in our land and took care of you when you left. We've seen his power and we've decided it would be wise to make an agreement with you. Promise not to hurt us. Don't you remember how good we were to you? We didn't hurt you. We let you leave Gerar in peace. And now it's plain to us that the Lord is blessing you."

Isaac prepared a feast, and they ate and drank together. The next morning they promised each other to remain at peace. They said good-bye and parted as friends.

# 15

# Jacob Steals Esau's Blessing

*Genesis 26 and 27*

ISAAC, an old man now, sat by the entrance of his tent. The morning sun was shining in his face, but he didn't mind. Isaac was blind. Old age had dimmed his eyes so he could no longer see the shepherds and the herdsmen as they took the animals out to graze. But he could hear them calling to each other, and he could pick out the sounds of the different animals. He could feel the pleasant heat on the top of his head, and he could smell the warm earth beneath his feet.

The Lord had richly blessed Isaac. He remembered how much Abraham and Sarah had loved him, and how Abraham had left him animals, silver, gold, and servants. The Lord had found Rebecca to be his wife. The Lord gave them not one, but two sons. He would be leaving all that he had to his sons, Esau and Jacob. With the Lord's help, he had lived in peace with his neighbors. Soon he would die, and his older son would take his place.

Isaac had only one disappointment. Esau had married Canaanite women. The Canaanites did not serve God. Yet the big hairy hunter was still his favorite son. It was time they had a talk.

"Son!"

"Yes, Father!"

"Come over here and listen to me!"

Esau came to Isaac's tent.

"I'm so old that I may die soon. Do one last thing for me. Get your bow and arrows and go out and hunt some wild game. Then cook the meat in that special way I like. I'll eat it and give you my final blessing before I die."

Rebecca was outside the tent, listening as Isaac spoke. When Esau left to hunt, she went to find Jacob.

"Listen!" she said to him. "I just overheard your father talking to Esau. He asked him to get some wild meat. He wants Esau to cook it for him to eat. Then he will give Esau his last blessing before he dies."

She looked around and then lowered her voice.

"Now pay attention to me, Jacob. Go out to the goat herd and get me two fat young kids. I'll cook the baby goats the same way Esau makes that special hunter's stew your father likes so much. Then you take it to him—and he'll give you his blessing before he dies!"

"Oh, mother!" Jacob answered. "Esau is a hairy man and my skin is smooth! What if my father touches me? He'll know that I'm tricking him, and he'll give me his curses instead of his blessing!"

"Let me worry about that," she answered. "Just do as I say. Now go get the goats!"

Jacob went out to the pasture and found two fat little goats. He killed them and brought the meat and the skins back to his mother. She cooked the meat Isaac's favorite way, seasoning it to taste like wild game.

Then she found some of Esau's hunting clothes and gave them to Jacob. She put the pieces of hairy goatskin over his arms and hands and along the back of his neck. He didn't look at all like Esau, but he certainly smelled like a hunter!

She gave Jacob the bowl of meat and some bread, and he stepped out of her tent.

Isaac was sleeping when Jacob entered his tent.

"Father!"

"Yes?" He turned his head toward the entrance of the tent. "Which of my sons are you?"

Jacob tried to make his voice sound like his

brother's. "I'm Esau, your firstborn son. I did what you told me. Please sit up and eat some of this meat and give me your blessing."

"How did you get back so soon, my son?"

"The Lord your God helped me," Jacob answered.

Isaac seemed suspicious. "Come closer," he said. "Let me touch you. Are you really my son Esau?"

Jacob put the bowl down and went over to his father. Isaac felt his arms and hands and the back of his neck.

"Ah!" he said, "the voice is Jacob's, but the hands are Esau's!"

Just as he was about to pronounce the blessing, he asked again, "Are you really my son Esau?"

"Of course I am," Jacob answered.

"Then bring me the meat and let me eat it. When I'm finished I'll give you my blessing."

Jacob picked up the meat and the bread and served his father. The old man chewed slowly, enjoying every bite. Then he drank the wine Jacob gave him. Finally he wiped his mouth and said, "Come here and kiss me, my son."

As Jacob bent over to kiss him, Isaac smelled his clothes.

"Ah! My son smells rich and damp, like a field which the Lord has blessed!"

Then he put his hands on Jacob's head and gave the blessing.

"May God give you and your descendants rain from heaven and riches from the earth. May he give you plenty of grain and wine. Other nations will bow down to you. Your descendants will rule over your brother's descendants. Cursed be everyone who curses you, and blessed be everyone who blesses you."

As soon as the old man finished, Jacob got up and hurried out of the tent.

Isaac started to doze off again, when Esau came back from the hunting. He, too, had cooked a special meal to take to his father. He entered Isaac's tent just a few minutes after Jacob left.

"Please, Father," Esau said. "Sit up and eat this wild meat that I've killed and cooked for you. And then give me your blessing."

"Who's that?"

"Why, Esau, your firstborn son. Who else?"

Then Isaac began to tremble and shake all over. "If you're Esau, who hunted the wild game I finished eating just before you came in? I blessed him, and the blessing is his forever!"

When Esau heard his father's words, he cried out bitterly, like an animal pierced by a hunter's arrow. "Bless me, too, Father!" he begged.

"I can't," Isaac said. "Your brother came here and tricked me into giving him your blessing!"

"This is the second time he has cheated me," Esau said. "First he stole my birthright, and now he has taken my blessing! Oh, don't you have a blessing saved for me?"

"I've already made his descendants the masters of yours," Isaac answered. "I've given them all their relatives as servants. I've given him grain and wine. What else is left, my son?"

"Don't you have more than one blessing, Father? Bless me, too!"

Isaac said nothing, and Esau began to cry.

Finally Isaac spoke. He put one trembling hand on Esau's shoulder and the other on Esau's head.

"Your home will be far from the riches of the earth and far from the rain of heaven," he began. "You and your descendants will fight to survive, and your people will serve your brother's people. But the time will come when they will rise up and break free from their masters."

But Esau was not happy. He was angry with his brother Jacob for cheating him.

# Jacob's Stairway to Heaven

*Genesis 27—29*

**E**SAU was furious with his brother Jacob. He walked through the camp muttering to himself, "My father will die soon. Then I'll kill Jacob!"

When Rebecca heard what Esau was saying, she sent for Jacob.

"Listen! Your brother Esau wants to get even with you. He is angry that you took away both his birthright and his blessing. He says he's going to kill you!"

Rebecca pulled Jacob inside her tent. "Now,

then, do what I say. You'll have to get out of here. Go to my brother Laban in Haran and stay with him for a while—until your brother cools down and forgets what you've done. Then I'll send for you. You can't stay here. Think of me! If Esau kills you, he'll be executed for murder. I'd lose both my sons in the same day!"

Then Rebecca went into Isaac's tent, while Jacob waited outside.

"You know how those two Canaanite women have made life miserable for us," she told Isaac. "Esau married them and brought them here against our wishes. Well, what's to prevent our other son from doing the same thing? Then life really won't be worth living! Let's send Jacob to Haran, to my brother Laban. He can find a wife there."

Rebecca didn't mention the trick she and Jacob had just played, or Esau's murderous plans.

Isaac nodded to her and called for Jacob. Jacob stood before his father with his head bowed.

"Don't marry a Canaanite woman," Isaac said to his son. "Go at once to Haran, to the house of your grandfather Bethuel, and choose a wife there."

Did the old man guess the fear in Jacob's heart or the hatred in Esau's? Perhaps he was remembering how his father Abraham had sent to Haran for Rebecca. Perhaps he knew Jacob's fears and forgave him. Whatever he was thinking, he seemed at peace.

"May God Almighty bless you," Isaac said, reaching his hand out to his son. "And may he give you many descendants, so that you become the father of many nations."

The young man was kneeling now, and his father's hands were on his head.

"May he give you the blessing of Abraham, and may your descendants possess this land, which God gave to Abraham."

Jacob left his father's tent with tears in his eyes. He began walking north, toward Haran,

with nothing but the clothes on his back and a shepherd's staff in his hand.

Shortly after sunset he came to a lonely place in the hill country, a dry and rocky spot that seemed deserted. He decided to spend the night there. He took one of the stones which was lying on the ground and put it under his head for a pillow. Then he lay down to sleep.

That night Jacob had a strange and wonderful dream. He saw a stairway which reached from the earth all the way to heaven. He saw angels of God going up and down the stairs.

Then he dreamed he saw the Lord standing by him. The Lord said, "I am the Lord, the God of your grandfather Abraham and your father Isaac. I will give you and your descendants this land. Your descendants will number as many as the specks of dust of the earth. They'll spread out far and wide, in every direction. All the nations of the earth will pray to be blessed as you and your descendants are blessed. Remember, I am with you. I'll protect you wherever you go, and I'll bring you back to this land. I won't leave you without keeping these promises."

Jacob woke up. "Surely the Lord lives here," he said, "but I didn't know it!"

Suddenly he felt afraid. "What a place!" he whispered. "This is the house of God! And that stairway is the entrance to heaven!"

In the morning Jacob took the stone which he had used as a pillow and stood it upright in the ground. He poured oil over the top of it to dedicate it to God, and he called the place Bethel, which means "house of God."

"If God stays with me, if he protects me on my journey and gives me the food and clothing I need, if I return safely to my father's house— well, then the Lord will be my God!" Jacob said.

"I'll give you a tenth of everything that you give me," Jacob told God. Then he left Bethel and continued on his way north, toward Haran.

Jacob was traveling to the native land of his mother, Rebecca, where his grandparents, Abraham and Sarah, had come from. It was a foreign country to him.

One day a few weeks later, Jacob came upon a well out in a field. Three flocks of sheep were lying around it, looking hot and thirsty. A huge stone covered the mouth of the well.

Some shepherds were standing next to the well. Jacob greeted them and asked, "Friends, where are you from?"

"We're from Haran," they answered.

"Do you know Laban, of the family of Nahor?" Jacob asked.

"We do."

"Is he well?"

"He is," they replied.

Then one of the shepherds pointed to a woman coming toward them. "And here comes his daughter Rachel with his sheep."

"But it's still broad daylight," said Jacob. "It's

not time to gather in the flocks yet. Why don't you water them and let them graze some more?"

"We can't until all the shepherds get here," they answered. "That stone on top of the well is too heavy for one person to move. It takes all of us together to roll it off the mouth of the well. Only then can we water the flocks. So we have to wait for the others."

While they were talking, Rachel came up to the well with her father's sheep.

As soon as Jacob saw her, he stepped up to the well and pushed the stone away. Then he watered his uncle's sheep.

When he was finished, he went up to Rachel and kissed her. Then he cried tears of joy and told her who he was. She ran home to tell her father.

When Laban heard the news, he rushed out to meet Jacob. He hugged and kissed his nephew and took him back to their house. There Jacob told him everything that had happened.

"You can stay with us," said Laban. "Make yourself at home. After all, you're one of my relatives." So Jacob stayed with them.

# 17

# Two Tricks and a Contest

*Genesis 29—30*

JACOB soon became part of Laban's family. He helped his uncle look after the sheep and goats and he did other chores for him.

Laban had two daughters. The older one, Leah, had no sparkle in her eyes. But the younger daughter, Rachel, was graceful and beautiful. Jacob was in love with her.

About a month after Jacob arrived in Haran, Laban called him aside. "Jacob, you don't have to work for me without pay just because you're my nephew," he said. "Tell me what I should give you."

Jacob didn't hesitate. "I'll work for you for seven years if you let me marry your daughter Rachel," he answered.

"Well, I'd rather give her to you than to a stranger," his uncle answered. "Stay with us."

Jacob stayed and worked seven years for Rachel. To him they seemed like seven days, he loved her so much.

Finally he said, "Uncle Laban, the time is up. Let me marry your daughter."

Laban invited all their friends and relatives to a wedding feast.

That evening he took his daughter to Jacob. She was wearing a heavy bridal veil, and Jacob married her.

The next morning he looked at his bride in the daylight, without her veil. It was Leah!

"How could you do this to me?" he asked Laban. "Didn't I work for you for seven years for Rachel? Why have you tricked me?"

"I was just giving Leah her right as firstborn," Laban answered. "In our country it's the custom for the older daughter to marry before the younger one. I'll tell you what. Finish the week of wedding celebrations with Leah, and then I'll give you my other daughter, too.

"Of course, if you want two brides, you must give me two bridal payments. If you want to marry Rachel later this week, you must promise to work for me another seven years."

Jacob agreed, and at the end of the week he

married Rachel. Then he kept his promise and stayed in Haran, working for Laban seven more years.

Jacob loved Rachel more than Leah. When the Lord saw how unhappy this made Leah, he gave her a son, while Rachel had no children.

"See, a son! Now my husband will love me," Leah said, and she named her baby Reuben (meaning "See").

But Jacob still loved Rachel more.

Then Leah had another son, and she named this one Simeon (meaning "Heard"). "The Lord heard I was unloved," she said.

When she had a third son, she named him Levi (meaning "Attached"). "Surely, now my husband will feel attached to me!" she said.

But Jacob still preferred Rachel.

Leah had a fourth son. She named him Judah, ("Praise") and said, "Praise the Lord!" for she still hoped to win her husband's love.

Each time Leah had a baby, Rachel became more and more jealous. "Give me children or I shall die," she told Jacob.

He was angry with her. "Can I take God's place?" he asked. "The Lord is the one who gives life."

"Then take my maid Bilhah and make her your wife," said Rachel. "She can have children, and they'll count as mine."

So Jacob took Bilhah as his wife, and she had a son. "God has been just!" said Rachel, and she named the child Dan ("Justice").

Then Bilhah had another son, and Rachel named this one Naphtali ("Fighting"). "I'm fighting in a hard contest with my sister," she said, "and I'm winning!"

When Leah realized what Rachel was up to, she did the same thing. She gave her maid Zilpah to Jacob as a wife. When Zilpah had a son, Leah named him Gad ("Lucky"). "Now I'm the lucky one!" she said.

Then Zilpah had another son, and Leah named him Asher ("Happy"). "How happy I am!" she said.

Leah was even happier when she had three more children herself. She named the boys Issachar ("Reward") and Zebulun ("Honor") and the girl, Dinah. "God has rewarded me with good gifts for my husband," she said. "Now he'll honor me!"

But then God answered Rachel's prayers and gave her a child of her own. "God has taken away my disgrace," she said, and named him Joseph ("Takes Away").

Soon after the birth of Joseph, Jacob said to Laban, "Let me go home now. Give me my wives and my twelve children. I've kept my promise; I've worked hard for you."

"Wait a minute," answered Laban. "Don't go. Listen to me. I just had my fortune told. It's because of you that God has blessed me. I'll pay you whatever you want if you stay."

"Yes, the Lord has blessed you since I've been here," Jacob answered. "You have much larger flocks than you did when I first came. But I have four wives and twelve children to take care of. It's time for me to work for them."

"What do you want?"

"Well," Jacob answered, "if you give me some animals of my own, I'll keep on working for you. Let me go through your whole flock today and pick out all the black sheep and all the striped and spotted goats. Give them to me as pay. It will be easy for you to check my honesty. If you find any light-colored animals in my flock, they're yours."

"All right," said Laban. "It's a deal."

Since most of Laban's animals were white, Jacob wasn't asking for much. But that same day Laban sneaked out to the pasture and took all the black sheep and all the striped and spotted goats and gave them to his sons. By the time Jacob checked the flock, there were none left for him.

But this time he didn't complain to Laban about the trick. He had a plan.

When the time came for the animals to breed and have babies, Jacob mated the male and female sheep so that all the strong, healthy ones had black lambs. He mated the male and female goats so that all the strong, healthy ones had striped and spotted kids. He kept these animals separate from Laban's. As they grew, he mated them again, and soon he had a large flock of strong, healthy, dark-colored animals, and Laban had a small flock of weak, unhealthy, light-colored ones.

For six more years Jacob worked for Laban. Every year his flock got bigger, and Laban's got smaller.

Jacob became a rich man with large flocks of sheep and goats, camels and donkeys, and servants of his own. God was keeping his promise to bless Jacob.

# 18

# Jacob Escapes from His Uncle

*Genesis 31*

LABAN'S sons were jealous of Jacob. The richer their cousin became, the more they complained about him. They told everyone that Jacob was wealthy because he had stolen their father's property. Jacob noticed that Laban himself seemed much less friendly.

About this time the Lord talked to Jacob in a dream. "I've seen what Laban has done to you, and I've made your flocks grow larger," he told Jacob. "I am the God you met at Bethel, where you anointed the pillar and vowed to serve me.

Now leave this country and go back to Canaan. I'll be with you."

Jacob sent a message to Rachel and Leah. He told them to meet him out in the pasture, where nobody but the sheep and goats could see and hear them.

"Your father doesn't like me anymore." he explained. "You know how hard I've worked for him, and how he played tricks on me. He sneaked off with my animals. But the God of my father has been with me and he has helped me. God showed me how to mate the animals so they would have strong, healthy, dark-colored babies. That's how my flock grew larger and larger, and your father's grew smaller and smaller. Your father agreed to give me all the dark-colored animals. And when he tried to trick me, God took your father's animals and gave them to me. For six years now the Lord has been building up my flocks.

"And now God has given me a message in a dream," Jacob continued. "He told me to leave this country and go back to the land where I was born."

"We're going with you!" said Rachel and Leah. "What's the use of staying here? Our father ignores our rights and treats us like foreigners. Everything God has taken from him should be ours anyway. When our father cheated you, he cheated us, too. Go on, do whatever God says!"

Then they all agreed to pretend that nothing

111

unusual was going on. They didn't tell Laban about their plans.

Soon it was sheep-shearing time, and Laban went away for three days to watch over the cutting of the wool. They decided to act.

Jacob put his children and his wives on camels, and they all rode off with the flocks and their servants. Soon they were on the other side of the Euphrates River and heading south toward the hill country of Gilead.

Before she left, Rachel took her father's household idols. These little clay figures were important to Laban. According to the law of Haran, whoever owned them had the right to all the family property.

Three days later Laban came home and discovered that Jacob had escaped. He called together all his men and chased after him.

By the seventh day Laban had nearly caught up with Jacob. But that night God spoke to him in a dream. "Be careful how you treat Jacob," he warned.

The next day Laban found Jacob's tents pitched in the hill country of Gilead. "What do you mean by tricking me?" he demanded. "You took my daughters away like prisoners of war! Why did you sneak away like that without telling me?

"I would have given you a farewell party," he continued. "We could have had a feast with music and singing! But you didn't even give me a chance to kiss my daughters and grandchildren good-bye. What a stupid way to leave!"

"I was afraid," Jacob answered. "I thought you might take your daughters away from me by force."

"Well, see here," said Laban. "I've got my men with me. I could hurt all of you if I wanted to. But last night in a dream the God of your father told me to be careful with you. All right then, go back where you came from. I understand. You're homesick. But why did you steal my gods?"

"I don't know anything about your idols," said Jacob. "If you find them on anyone here, let the thief die! Our relatives can be witnesses. If you find anything here that belongs to you, take it!"

Jacob had no idea that Rachel had stolen the idols. He understood the law, though, and he knew why Laban was so upset. If Jacob had the idols, then all Laban's family property was his.

Laban went into Jacob's tent and searched through it. Then he looked through Bilhah's tent and Zilpah's tent and Leah's tent. He found nothing.

He walked from Leah's tent to Rachel's.

While Laban was in the other tents, Rachel had stuffed the idols into a camel saddle. She was sitting on top of them when he entered.

"Excuse me, Father," she said. "Please don't be offended if I don't get up to greet you. I'm not feeling well today."

Laban looked through everything in her tent and found nothing. He went outside where Jacob was waiting.

"What have I done to deserve such treatment?" he asked. "You've searched through all the tents and you haven't found a thing, have you? Come on, show us! Put everything you've found out here in front of all these people! Come on, Laban!"

Laban had nothing to show.

"After all the years I've worked for you, look at how you treat me!" Jacob complained. "Twenty years taking care of your animals, and I never took a thing that didn't belong to me. I never ate one of your rams. I even paid for the animals that were killed by wild beasts. It wasn't easy work. I had to put up with the burning heat by day and the frost by night. Sometimes I could hardly sleep. For twenty years I worked—fourteen years for your daughters and six years for the flock—and you kept playing tricks on me. If the God of my grandfather Abraham and my father Isaac hadn't been with me, you would have sent me away empty-handed! But God saw my trouble. He knew how hard I worked. That's why he told you last night to leave me alone."

"These women are my daughters and these children are my grandchildren," Laban replied. "The animals are mine, too. All this belongs to me." He had given up hope of finding the idols, and he knew he had no claim to the property. "What can I do? Would I hurt my family? Come now, let's make an agreement."

Jacob agreed to make a peace treaty with Laban. He took a large stone and set it up. Then he told his men to gather stones. He piled them next to the pillar.

"This pile of stones will be our witness," said Laban. "It will stand like a watchtower. May God watch between us when we're out of each other's sight. I won't pass beyond these stones to attack you, and don't you pass over to this side to attack me. May the God of Abraham and the god of

Nahor keep peace between us."

Then Jacob made a vow in the name of the God of Isaac that he wouldn't cross beyond the pile of stones to attack Laban. He offered a sacrifice and invited Laban and his men to a feast. They ate and spent the night there in the hills of Gilead.

The next morning Laban kissed his daughters and grandchildren good-bye and went back to Haran.

Jacob and his wives and children, his servants, and his animals, continued on their way.

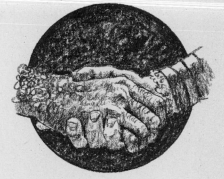

# 19

# The Mysterious Wrestling Match

*Genesis 32—33*

**A**FTER his escape from Laban, Jacob continued his journey south with his family. On the way, angels of God came to meet him.

When he saw them, Jacob said, "This must be God's army camp," and he named the place Mahanaim, meaning "camps."

Surely the Lord was still with him! But Jacob was worried about meeting his brother Esau. Twenty years ago Esau wanted to murder Jacob. What would happen now?

Jacob decided to send messengers on ahead to Esau, who was living in Edom, southeast of Canaan. He said to the messengers, "Tell Esau that I've been staying with Laban until recently. Tell him I own many cattle and donkeys, sheep and goats, and I have many servants. I want to let him know I'm coming so he'll be friendly to us."

The messengers took Jacob's message to Esau and then returned to Jacob.

"We met your brother," they said. "He's already on the way to meet you, and he has four hundred men with him."

Jacob was frightened. Four hundred men!

He divided his people into two groups. If Esau attacked one group, maybe the other could escape.

Then he prayed, "O God of my grandfather Abraham and my father Isaac, you told me to go back to my own country. You promised to be good to me. I'm not worthy of all the kindness you've shown me so faithfully. Twenty years ago I left home with nothing but the staff in my hand, and now look at me! I have wives and children and all this property.

"Save me, I pray, from my brother Esau," Jacob continued. "I'm afraid that he's coming to kill me, and these mothers and children, too! But you promised you'd be good to me. You said you'd give me as many descendants as there are grains of sand on the seashore."

Jacob and his family spent the night there at Mahanaim.

The next day Jacob went through the flocks and picked out some of each kind of animal. He would give Esau five hundred animals as a present. He told his servants, "Take these animals and go ahead of me. When you meet my brother, tell him that all these animals belong to me. They're a present for him. Tell him that Jacob is right behind you."

He thought, "If I give Esau these gifts first, if he sees the sheep and the goats, the cattle, the camels, and the donkeys—if he sees all this before he sees me, perhaps by the time we meet he may be ready to forgive me."

So Jacob sent the servants with the animals on ahead and he spent a second night there.

During the night Jacob got up and led his wives and children to a place where they could cross the Jabbok River. After they were safely across, he stood alone on the bank of the stream.

Suddenly a man came up to him in the dark. The man grabbed Jacob and began to wrestle with him. They struggled together through the night.

When he saw that he couldn't keep Jacob down, the man hit Jacob's hip and knocked it out of joint. Then he told Jacob, "Let me go. It's almost morning."

Jacob answered, "I won't let you go until you bless me."

"What's your name?" the man asked.

"Jacob."

"You shall no longer be called Jacob. From now on your name is Israel (meaning "Wrestler with God"), for you have struggled with God and with man, and you have won."

"Who are you? Please tell me your name," said Jacob.

"You must not ask my name," said the stranger. Then he blessed Jacob and left.

Jacob named that place Penuel, meaning "The Face of God."

"I've seen God face-to-face," Jacob said, "and my life has been spared."

The sun was rising over Penuel as Jacob limped away, leaning on one hip. He was a changed person now. He had met God. Now he was ready to meet his brother.

Just as he reached his wives and children, Jacob saw Esau coming toward him with the four hundred men. Quickly Jacob divided his children among Leah, Rachel, and the two maidservants. He put the maids and their children first, Leah and her children next, and Rachel and Joseph last. Then Jacob limped on ahead of them, bowing low seven times as he approached his brother.

Esau ran out to meet him. He hugged Jacob and threw his arms around his neck and kissed him. They both cried. Then Esau saw the women and children. "Who are these people with you?" he asked.

"They're the children whom God has given to me," Jacob answered.

Then Jacob's wives and children went up to Esau, bowing low, the maidservants and their children first, then Leah and her children, and last Rachel and Joseph.

"What are all those animals that I met just now?" Esau asked.

"My gifts to you, to please you, sir," Jacob answered.

"Brother, I have plenty!" Esau laughed. "Keep them for yourself!"

"No, please take them," said Jacob. "You don't know how happy I am to see you face-to-face. I was afraid of you. Please take my presents, for God has been good to me and I have many more."

And since Jacob kept pressing the gifts on him, Esau accepted them.

"Let's go," Esau said. "No use staying around here. Come on, let's go back to Edom together!"

"Oh, no," answered Jacob. He was relieved to find his brother friendly, but he didn't want to go with him. "You see how frail the children are, and how slowly the animals move along. You go on ahead, and I'll come more slowly with the children. We'll meet you in Edom."

"Well, then," said Esau, "as you like. But let me at least leave some of my men as guides."

"Oh, no," said Jacob. "That's not necessary. Please."

So Esau started back to Edom that same day

without Jacob. (He lived there the rest of his life and was the ancestor of twelve tribes of Edom.)

When Esau and his men were out of sight, Jacob and his family headed in the opposite direction, to Succoth.

Jacob's family stayed a while in Succoth. He built shelters there for himself and the animals. Then they pulled up their tent pegs and moved to Shechem, on the other side of the Jordan River, in the land of Canaan.

Jacob pitched his tents outside the city of Shechem and built an altar to the God of Israel.

# The Story of Joseph and His Brothers

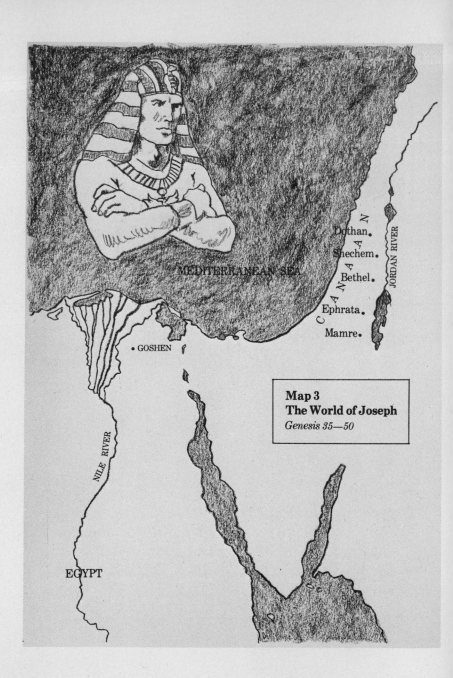

Map 3
The World of Joseph
*Genesis 35—50*

MEDITERRANEAN SEA

C A N A A N

JORDAN RIVER

Dothan.
Shechem.
Bethel.
Ephrata.
Mamre.

• GOSHEN

NILE RIVER

EGYPT

# 20

# Joseph Sold into Slavery

*Genesis 35—37*

ONE day while Jacob was still living in Shechem, God told him to take his family to Bethel. He was to build an altar there, at the place where he had met the Lord and had seen the stairway to heaven many years ago. The family cleaned up and got rid of their idols. Then they went to Bethel, built an altar, and prayed to the God who had helped Jacob. Then they headed south.

Rachel was expecting a child, and on the way she gave birth to a baby boy. As the baby was born, Rachel died. Jacob buried her there beside the road to Ephrata, and set up a monument of stones on her grave. Then he continued on to Mamre, where he and his family settled.

Jacob missed Rachel terribly. He could see her face every time he looked at her sons, seventeen-year-old Joseph and baby Benjamin. He loved them more than any of his other children.

Sometimes Joseph went out with his older brothers to help take care of their father's flocks. His brothers knew that he watched them and told their father bad things about them.

To show his great love for Joseph, Jacob made him a long robe with long full sleeves and decorated it with many-colored embroidery. When Joseph's older brothers saw this fancy coat, they hated him so much that they couldn't even say a kind word to him.

One time Joseph had a strange dream.

"Listen!" he said to his brothers. "Let me tell you about my dream! I dreamed we were all out in the field tying up bundles of wheat. Suddenly my sheaf rose and stood up straight. Then your sheaves formed a circle around my sheaf and bowed down to it!"

"What are you talking about?" they said. "Do you think you're going to be a king and rule over us?" They hated Joseph even more because of his talk about the dream.

Then Joseph had another dream, and he told them about it. "Listen!" he said again. "I've had another dream! This time the sun and the moon and eleven stars were bowing down to me!"

They gave him a rude answer and turned away.

He went to his father and told him about the dream.

"What kind of dream is that?" Jacob scolded. "Do you really think our whole family is going to c ..1e and bow down to you?"

But while the brothers were angry and jealous, Jacob kept thinking about Joseph's dream and wondering what it meant.

One day Jacob called Joseph to his tent. "Your brothers have gone to Shechem to find pasture for my flocks," he said. "I want you to go to them. See how they are doing, and check on the animals."

"I'm ready to go!" said Joseph.

"Well, get your robe and be off. After you've seen them, come right back and tell me how things are." Then he sent Joseph on his way.

When he got to Shechem, Joseph couldn't find his brothers anywhere. He wandered through the fields looking for them.

Finally he met a man who told him that they had left Shechem for Dothan. So Joseph walked north through the hills, toward Dothan.

Before he reached them, Joseph's older brothers saw him coming through the fields. "Here comes that dreamer!" one of them said.

"Come on," said another. "Let's kill him now

and throw his body into one of these pits!" He pointed toward a deep hole in the ground, a cistern dug to store water in the wilderness.

"We can say that a wild animal attacked him," another brother suggested. "Then we'll see what happens to those dreams of his!"

Reuben, the oldest brother, didn't like this plotting against Joseph. "Let's not kill him!" he said. He thought quickly. Perhaps he could save Joseph. "Just throw him into the pit alive," he suggested. He planned to return later, when the others were gone, rescue Joseph, and take him to their father.

Just then Joseph arrived. The brothers grabbed the boy and ripped off his long beautiful robe, the one that Jacob had given him. Then they threw him into the pit.

The pit was empty. There was no water in it, but it was very deep, and Joseph couldn't get out. He called to his brothers, crying and begging them to pull him out, but they ignored him. Instead, they sat down to eat their lunch on the grass.

Reuben got up and went off by himself to another part of the field. He had no appetite.

While the others were still eating, they saw a caravan of camels going by. It was a group of traders going from Gilead to Egypt with a load of perfumes and spices.

Judah remembered that such traders would buy and sell anything. "What good would it do to

kill Joseph and cover up the murder?" he asked.
"Come on, let's sell him to these traders. Then we
wouldn't have to kill him. After all, he is our
brother, our own flesh and blood!"

The others agreed, and they pulled Joseph out
of the pit. Then they stopped the caravan and

sold Joseph to the traders for twenty pieces of silver.

After the caravan disappeared, Reuben came back and looked into the pit. "The boy's not there!" he cried. "What am I going to do?"

They told him their plan.

One of the brothers killed a baby goat, and another dipped Joseph's robe in the blood. Then they returned home and showed the bloody robe to Jacob. "We found this in the wilderness," they said. "Does it belong to your son?"

Jacob lifted the long sleeves and felt the beautiful embroidery. "My son's robe!" he cried. "A wild beast has eaten him! Joseph has been torn to pieces by wild animals!"

Then he tore off his clothes and put on sackcloth, the clothes for mourning. He sat in his tent crying. Jacob wouldn't come out or talk to anyone for many days.

All his children tried to comfort him, but Jacob refused to be comforted. "No," he said, "leave me alone. I'll go to my grave mourning for my son!"

# Joseph Thrown into Prison

*Genesis 39—40*

THE traders sold Joseph as a slave to Potiphar, a high official of Pharaoh, the king of Egypt. Even though he was far from his home and family, Joseph knew that the Lord was with him. He knew that God was watching over him and taking care of him every day.

Potiphar put Joseph to work as a house slave. He soon noticed that the Lord gave Joseph success in everything he did. Potiphar was so pleased that he made Joseph his personal servant. He put Joseph in charge of his whole house and everything in it.

The Lord blessed the house of Potiphar because of Joseph. He blessed everything Potiphar owned, inside and out.

Potiphar's wife liked the handsome young man who was in charge of the house and all the other servants. She asked him to join her in cheating Potiphar. But Joseph refused. Potiphar trusted him, Joseph explained, and to hurt him would be a sin against God.

Day after day she kept on teasing him, but Joseph tried to ignore her. One day when Joseph went into the house to do his work, nobody else was around. Potiphar's wife grabbed him by his cloak. He ran outside, leaving his cloak in her hand.

"Help! Help!" she screamed.

The other servants came running, and she showed them Joseph's cloak.

"Look!" she cried. "That Hebrew fellow attacked me! When he heard me calling for help, he left his cloak here and ran outside!"

She told Potiphar the same story when he came home. He was so angry that he had Joseph arrested and put in prison.

Even in prison the Lord was with Joseph. He showed his kindness toward him by causing the warden to take a liking to Joseph. The warden put Joseph in charge of all the other prisoners. Since the Lord was with Joseph, everything he did turned out well, even in prison.

One day two new prisoners were put in the same jail. They were servants from Pharaoh's palace, sent to prison because Pharaoh was angry with them. One was the chief butler, who served Pharaoh's wine. The other was the chief baker, who made Pharaoh's bread. Joseph was put in charge of both of them.

One morning Joseph noticed that the butler and the baker seemed sad. He asked them, "Why do you look so gloomy today?"

"Each of us had a strange dream last night," they answered. "Nobody here can tell us what our dreams mean."

"God gives the ability to understand dreams," Joseph said. "Tell me your dreams."

So the butler told Joseph his dream. "In my dream I saw a grapevine with three branches," he began. "The vine started to grow. First the leaves came out, then the blossoms, and finally the grapes. In the dream I was standing by Pharaoh's table. I was holding his wine cup in my hand. I reached out and picked the grapes and squeezed them until his cup was full. Then I gave the cup to Pharaoh."

"Here's what your dream means," said Joseph. "The three branches are three days. In three days Pharaoh will release you from prison and put you back in your old job. You'll stand by his table and give him his wine cup, just as before."

The butler was smiling.

"But please remember me when everything is going well for you again," Joseph said. "Please be kind enough to mention me to Pharaoh. Help me get out of this place, too. After all, I was stolen from my home and sold as a slave. Then I was put in this dungeon even though I haven't done anything to deserve such treatment!"

The baker spoke up. "It's my turn now." He was hoping his dream had a pleasant meaning, too.

"Let me tell you my dream," he said. "I was

carrying three baskets on top of my head. In the top basket were all kinds of baked goods for Pharaoh. It was filled with bread and rolls and buns and cakes. But birds came down and pecked at the baked goods and ate everything in the basket."

Joseph looked at the baker sadly. "This is what your dream means," he said. "The three baskets are three days. In three days Pharaoh will take you from this prison to be hanged. And when you're dead, the birds will come down and peck at your body."

Everything happened just as Joseph said. Three days later was Pharaoh's birthday, and he gave a banquet for all his officials. He ordered his guards to take the butler and the baker out of prison. He brought the butler back to the palace and gave him his old job of waiting on Pharaoh's table again. But he sent the baker out to be hanged and left his body for the birds to peck to pieces.

Everything was going well for the butler again. But he never thought of Joseph. He forgot all about him.

# A Slave Becomes Ruler of Egypt

*Genesis 41*

**T**WO years passed. The chief butler was in the palace and Joseph was still in prison. One morning as the butler was standing by Pharaoh's table, he heard Pharaoh tell about two strange dreams he had the night before. Pharaoh was so worried about the dreams that he had sent for all his magicians and wise men. None of them could tell Pharaoh what the dreams meant.

Then the butler remembered his own strange dream, and he spoke up. "Let me make a confession," he said to Pharaoh. "Two years ago you were angry with me and the chief baker. You put us in prison. While we were there, we both had a dream the same night. A young Hebrew prisoner told us what our dreams meant. And each dream turned out just as he said!"

Pharaoh sent for Joseph right away. The guards rushed him from prison, told him to shave his beard, and gave him new clothes to put on. Then they brought him to the palace to see Pharaoh.

"I've had two strange dreams," Pharaoh told Joseph. "None of these wise men and magicians can tell me what my dreams mean. But I'm sure there's an important message in them. I understand that you can tell the meaning of dreams."

"No, sir," answered Joseph. "I can't do that. But God will tell us what they mean."

Then Pharaoh told Joseph his dreams. "In my first dream I was standing on the bank of the Nile," he said. "I saw seven beautiful fat cows come from the river to graze on the reed grass. Then right behind them seven more cows came from the river. But these cows were thin and bony and ugly. I've never seen such ugly cows in all of Egypt!

"The thin and ugly cows ate up the seven healthy ones," Pharaoh continued. "Yet even after they ate them, they looked just as bad as before! Well, then I woke up.

"Soon I fell asleep again, and I had another

dream. I dreamed I saw seven heads of grain, large and healthy, all growing from one stalk of wheat. But right behind them were seven other heads of grain, thin and unhealthy, withered from the hot desert wind. Then I dreamed that the seven thin heads of grain swallowed up the seven healthy ones!"

Joseph was listening carefully.

"I've told these dreams to all the magicians and wise men of Egypt," Pharaoh said, "but none of them can tell me what they mean."

"Both of Pharaoh's dreams have the same meaning," said Joseph. "God is telling you what he's going to do. The dreams are messages from God."

Then he explained to Pharaoh what the dreams meant. "The seven fat cows are seven years. So are the seven healthy heads of grain. They both mean the same thing. The seven thin and ugly cows and the seven withered heads of grain are seven years, too.

"God has shown you what's going to happen," Joseph continued. "Just ahead are seven years of good, healthy crops. There will be seven years of great plenty in the land of Egypt. But these good years will be followed by seven years of famine, seven years with no crops at all. The seven good years will be forgotten because of the seven bad years. The land will be ruined by the terrible famine.

"You had two dreams with the same message

because God has already decided what he's going to do," Joseph told Pharaoh. "You must get ready, for soon your dreams will come true. Find a wise man. Put him in charge of the land to gather food during the seven good years and store it in the towns. Then when the seven years of famine come, you'll be prepared. You'll have enough food saved to feed the people. If you do this, your country will be saved."

Pharaoh and all his officials were pleased with Joseph. "We'll never find a wiser man than Joseph," Pharaoh said. "He has the Spirit of God in him."

Then he turned to Joseph. "Since God has told all this to you, you must be wiser than anyone else. I'll put you in charge of the land. All the people will obey your orders. Only I will be above you."

He took off his signet ring, the one engraved with the royal seal. "See, I place you in charge of the whole land of Egypt," he said. And he put the ring on Joseph's finger.

Then he had Joseph dressed in fine linen robes, and he placed a gold chain around his neck. He gave Joseph a royal chariot to ride through the land, and servants to run in front so that people would not get in his way.

"No one in the land of Egypt will do a thing without your permission," said Pharaoh. "You are ruler of all the land." Then he gave Joseph an Egyptian name and an Egyptian wife.

The next seven years were years of great plenty, just as God had said. The land of Egypt produced more crops than the people could use. The grain was full and healthy, and the animals grew fat and beautiful. No one had ever seen such abundance.

Joseph traveled through the land in his chariot, collecting grain and storing it in the towns. There was as much wheat as sand on the seashore. After a while he had to stop measuring it.

During these years Joseph and his Egyptian wife, Asenath, had two sons. "God has made me forget all my trouble and my boyhood home," said Joseph. So he named his first son Manasseh, which means "Forgetting."

When his second son was born, Joseph said, "God has made me fruitful and he has given me children in the land of my trouble." He named his second son Ephraim, which means "Fruitful."

Then the seven years of plenty were over. The seven years of famine began, just as Joseph had said.

It was a terrible famine. The grain was thin and unhealthy. The hot wind blew from the eastern desert and withered the wheat on the stalks. The animals had nothing to eat. They became thin and bony and terrible looking.

The Egyptian people were so hungry they cried to Pharaoh for food. He told them to go to Joseph. Joseph opened up the storehouses and sold grain to the Egyptians.

The famine was so bad that it spread to other countries. Only in the land of Egypt was there enough food. When people came to Egypt from other countries, Joseph sold them food. The next year the famine grew worse.

# The Brothers Go To Egypt

*Genesis 42*

JACOB and his family were hungry. The terrible famine had reached Canaan. Every day the grass became drier and the sheep and goats thinner. Many had already died.

The people in Jacob's tents were weak. They sat quietly all day, with dull eyes and thin faces. There was no use doing anything. They were dying.

Then one day Jacob heard from some passing travelers that there was food for sale in Egypt.

"Why do you sit there just staring at each

other?" he said to his sons. "Do something! I hear there's food in Egypt. Go down and buy some for us, so we don't all starve to death!"

"Can't I go, too, Father?" asked Benjamin as his older brothers prepared for the trip to Egypt. "There's nothing to do around here!"

"No, my son. You stay here with me." Jacob remembered how Joseph had gone to Shechem and how he had never come back. He remembered Rachel dying on the road to Ephrata. He hugged Benjamin. With Rachel and Joseph gone, he

loved Benjamin more than anyone or anything in the world.

Jacob's ten older sons made their way to Egypt. They joined the other hungry people standing in line outside the place where the ruler was selling grain.

When it was their turn, they came before a clean-shaven Egyptian about forty years old. The man was dressed in fine white linen and wearing a gold necklace and the royal signet ring. They didn't recognize their brother Joseph. They bowed low before him, with their faces to the ground.

When Joseph saw the ten bearded Hebrews in their striped woolen cloaks bowing before him, he remembered the dreams he had had many years earlier. He recognized his brothers, but he decided not to tell them who he was.

Speaking harshly and using the Egyptian language, Joseph asked them, "Where do you come from?"

"From the land of Canaan, to buy food," they answered in Hebrew.

Joseph continued speaking to them in Egyptian, pretending that he didn't understand their language.

"You're spies," he said. "You've come to Egypt to see how weak we are!"

"No, sir," one of them answered. "We're really here to buy food, sir. We're brothers, not a gang of spies. We're honest men!"

"No," said Joseph, "I can tell. You're spies. You came to check on the weakness of our land!"

"We're from a family of twelve brothers, sir!" they said. "We're sons of the same man in the land of Canaan. The youngest brother is home with our father, and another brother is dead."

"I don't believe a word you're saying," Joseph said. "You're spies. If you're honest men, prove it. Bring your youngest brother here to me. If you don't, as surely as Pharaoh lives, you'll all stay here!" He sounded so much like an Egyptian official they never suspected he was Joseph.

"Send someone back to get your younger brother," Joseph continued, "and the rest of you stay here under guard. That's how I'll find out whether you're telling the truth. If you can't prove your story, then I say you're a gang of spies!"

The brothers cried and begged Joseph to believe their story, but he ignored them. He ordered the guards to throw them all into prison for three days.

On the third day he sent for them and said, "If you do as I say, I'll let you live, for I fear and obey God. Here's a chance to prove yourselves. I'll keep one of you here. The rest of you may go back with food for your family. But you must bring your youngest brother to me. That will show that you've been telling the truth, and I won't have you killed."

They agreed to do as he said. Then they turned

to each other and began to talk among themselves. They didn't know that Joseph understood every word they were saying.

"What can we do?" asked one. "We're being punished for what we did to our brother Joseph more than twenty years ago!"

"Yes," agreed another. "We watched him suffer. He begged us to pull him out of the pit, but we wouldn't listen!"

"That's why this terrible thing is happening to us," said another brother.

"Didn't I warn you not to hurt him?" asked Reuben. "But you wouldn't listen! Now we're being paid back for causing his death!"

Joseph turned away from them with tears in his eyes. When he was able to speak again, he told his guards to take Simeon, the second oldest brother, and tie him up right there in front of the others.

Then he ordered his servants to fill the men's sacks with grain and to put their money in the sacks. He gave them food for their journey and watched while they loaded their donkeys and left the city.

That night when the nine brothers made camp, one of them opened his sack to get food for his donkey. He saw that his money was there in the mouth of the sack.

"Someone has returned my money!" he called out to his brothers. "It's here in my sack!"

They looked at the money. Fearfully they

asked each other, "What is God doing to us?"

They were afraid to return to Egypt, where Simeon was a prisoner, so they continued on to Canaan.

When they arrived home, they told their father what had happened and how the ruler of Egypt had accused them of spying. They explained how Simeon had been tied up and how they had promised to come back with Benjamin.

Then as they emptied the grain out of their sacks, they found their money. Each one's money was in his own sack!

When they saw the money, they and their father were afraid.

"Do you want me to lose all my children?" asked Jacob. "Joseph is gone; Simeon is gone; and now you want to take Benjamin away from me! Haven't I suffered enough?"

"I'll make sure Benjamin comes back," said Reuben. "If anything happens to your son Benjamin, you can kill my two sons! Let me take care of him. I promise to bring him home safe and sound!"

"No!" cried Jacob. "I won't let you! You can't take Benjamin to Egypt. Joseph is dead and Benjamin is all I have left of Rachel's children. If anything happens to him, I'll go to my grave with sorrow."

Jacob hugged Benjamin close to him. He wasn't going to let his youngest son out of his sight.

**24**

# Joseph Tests His Brothers

*Genesis 43—45*

THE famine in Canaan grew worse and worse. Jacob's large family soon ate all the food his sons had brought back from Egypt and there was nothing left.

Jacob called his sons together. "Go back and buy more food," he told them.

"Father, remember what we told you?" said Judah. "The ruler of Egypt warned us not to come back without Benjamin. We'll go to Egypt and get food for you, but only if you're ready to let us take him with us. If you won't let him go, it's no use. The man told us not to return without Benjamin.

"Oh, why do you make it so hard for me?" asked Jacob. "Why did you tell him you had another brother?"

"We didn't mean any harm," one of the brothers answered.

"He kept asking us questions about ourselves and our family," another one remembered. " 'Is your father still living?' 'Do you have another brother?' We had to answer!"

"How were we to know that he would tell us to bring Benjamin there?" asked another.

Then Judah said, "Send the boy with me. We'd better leave right away, or we'll starve. I'll take care of him. If anything happens to Benjamin, you can blame me. Now, come on! We've waited long enough. Let's get going. If we hadn't wasted all this time, we could have been there and back twice by now!"

"If that's how it must be, let's make the best of it," said Jacob. "Take some presents with you to give to that Egyptian. Perhaps when he sees the presents he'll be friendly. Take some of the best things from Canaan—some perfumes, a little honey, some spices, and some pistachio nuts and almonds."

The old man was thinking carefully. "This time take twice as much money as before. You must pay back the money that you found in your sacks." He sighed. "Perhaps that was a mistake."

Then he limped over to his son Benjamin and hugged him.

"Take your brother and go," he told the others. He was crying. "Go back to that Egyptian. And may God Almighty make him have mercy on you, so he'll set Simeon free and let Benjamin come back to me." He let go of Benjamin. "As for me, if I'm to lose my children, I'll lose them." He limped back to his tent, not watching them as they got ready to leave.

Then the brothers took the gifts and the money and Benjamin and set out for Egypt and the man who was selling grain.

They arrived in Egypt and went straight to Joseph. When he saw them with Benjamin, he told his servant, "Take these men to my house and prepare a meal for them. They'll eat with me at noon."

The servant led the brothers to Joseph's house.

"What's this all about?" one of them asked.

"We're being brought here because of that money in our sacks," another one whispered.

"These Egyptians are going to attack us and take our donkeys and make us their slaves," warned another.

When they got to the door of Joseph's house, they spoke to the servant. "Please, sir," said one of the brothers. "We came here once before to buy food. But when we opened our sacks we found our money—the exact amount we had paid for the grain! So we've brought back that money, and enough extra money to buy more food. We don't know who put the money in our sacks."

"It's all right," said Joseph's servant. "Don't be afraid. It must have been your God, the God of your father, who put treasure in your sacks for you. I remember that you paid me for the food."

Then he went in and brought Simeon out to them.

Next he took the eleven brothers inside Joseph's house, gave them water to wash their feet, and got food for their donkeys. He told them to wait for his master, who was coming at noon to eat with them.

While they were waiting, they unpacked the presents and laid them out.

At noon Joseph came home and they gave him the gifts from their father. Then they bowed down before him.

He asked them how they were. Then he said, "How is your old father? Is he still alive and well?"

"Sir, our father is alive and well," they answered, kneeling down and bowing before him again.

Joseph looked at Benjamin, the son of his mother, Rachel. He hadn't seen him since Benjamin was a baby. "Is this the youngest brother, the one you told me about?" he asked.

They nodded.

"God be gracious to you, my boy," Joseph said.

Suddenly Joseph left the room. He felt so good

about seeing his brother that he couldn't hold back the tears. He went into his private room and cried. Then he washed his face and came back, in control of himself again. He ordered the servants to bring in the meal.

Joseph was served at one table and his brothers at another, because the Egyptians didn't eat with foreigners. He seated his brothers by their ages, from the oldest to the youngest.

When they saw how they were seated, the brothers looked at each other in astonishment. What strange power did this Egyptian have? How did he know the order of their ages?

When the servants brought the food, they gave Benjamin five times as much as the others. Joseph watched them carefully.

When they were finished, Joseph ordered his servant to fill their sacks with as much grain as they could carry and to put each man's money in the top of his sack. He told him to put his best silver cup in Benjamin's sack.

Early the next morning the eleven brothers loaded the sacks of grain onto their donkeys and began their journey home. Just as they got outside the city, Joseph's servant came riding up to them.

"Halt!" he ordered. "Why have you cheated my master after he was so kind to you? He told me to hurry after you and find the silver cup that you stole from him. Why did you do such a wicked thing?"

The brothers spoke eagerly, one after the other.

"What do you mean?"

"How can you say such things, sir?"

"We would never do such a thing!"

"In fact, we even brought back the money we found in our sacks the first time!"

"Why would we steal silver or gold from your master's house?"

"If any of us has it, sir, put him to death and make the rest of us your slaves!"

They were sure it was all a mistake.

"That sounds fair," answered Joseph's servant, "but only the one who has the silver cup will be taken. The rest of you will go free."

They quickly lowered their sacks, sure that there was nothing in them but grain. They opened them and let the servant search each carefully, beginning with Reuben and ending with Benjamin.

The silver cup was in Benjamin's sack.

When the brothers saw the cup, they cried out in horror and sorrow. Then they slowly loaded the sacks onto the donkeys again, turned around, and went back to the city.

They found Joseph still in his house and they threw themselves down before him.

"What have you done?" he asked. "Didn't you realize that I would catch you?"

Judah spoke. "What can we say, sir? How can we argue? How can we prove that we're innocent?

God is punishing us for our old crimes, sir. We're all your slaves, not just the one who had your cup."

"No," answered Joseph, "that won't do! I'll only punish him. He'll be my slave and the rest of you can go back to your father." He waited. What

would his brothers do? Would they leave Benjamin and go home without him?

Judah spoke again. "Please, sir, I beg you, let me speak. Please be patient with me, sir, you who are as great as Pharaoh.

"Sir, you asked us about our family, so we told you about our old father and his love for his two youngest sons. One of them is dead and only the youngest is left. Jacob loves him like his own life," Judah said. "You told us to bring the boy down here, even though we explained how hard it would be for our father to let him go. But we were hungry and our father told us to come back here to get more food. Oh, sir, if anything happens to Benjamin, our father will die of sorrow! His whole life is wrapped up in the boy."

Judah pleaded with the Egyptian. "I promised my life to my father for Benjamin! Let me stay here, sir! Let me be your slave! Take me and let the boy go home with the others! I can't go back to my father without Benjamin! I can't bear to see this terrible suffering come upon my father!"

Joseph couldn't control his feelings anymore. He ordered all the Egyptian servants to leave the room, and then he spoke to his brothers in their own language. "I'm Joseph!" he said. "Is Father still alive?"

His brothers were so shocked that they couldn't speak.

"Come close to me," he said.

As they gathered around him, he explained,

"I'm Joseph, your brother, whom you sold into slavery. But don't worry or blame yourselves. It was really God who sent me here ahead of you, to save lives. This is only the second year of the famine. There will be five more years of bad crops. God sent me ahead of you to rescue you, and to let you and your descendants live. Your lives have been saved in this astonishing way because it was really God who sent me here, not you."

His brothers were still staring at him, and Joseph went on. "God has made me Pharaoh's highest official. I'm ruler over this whole country, over all of Egypt. Now hurry back to my father and tell him everything I've said. Tell him to come to Egypt right away. You can all live near me in the Goshen area of Egypt—you and your children, your flocks, and your herds. I'll take care of all of you, for there are still five more years of famine coming.

"Can't you see? I'm really Joseph! Tell my father about me, how I'm the ruler of Egypt. But hurry now and bring him here!"

Then Joseph threw his arms around his brother Benjamin and cried, and Benjamin cried, too, and hugged him.

Still crying, Joseph hugged and kissed all his brothers. After that they all began to talk to him.

Pharaoh and the other officials were happy to hear Joseph's good news. Pharaoh told Joseph that his family was welcome to come and settle in Egypt.

Then Joseph gave his brothers wagons and food for the journey, and new clothes. He gave Benjamin three hundred pieces of silver and five sets of new clothes. He sent his father twenty donkeys loaded with the finest products of Egypt and food for the journey back. Then he sent them on their way, back to Jacob in Canaan.

When he heard that Joseph was still alive and ruling Egypt, Jacob fainted. He couldn't believe it.

They repeated everything that Joseph had said. They showed him the wagons and donkeys that Joseph had sent. Then he recovered from the shock.

"It's enough," he said. "My son Joseph is still alive! I must go and see him before I die."

# Jacob's Family Moves to Egypt

*Genesis 46—50*

JACOB'S family packed everything they owned into the wagons Joseph had sent from Egypt. His sons put Jacob and their children and their wives in the wagons. Then they herded their animals together and began the long walk from Canaan to Egypt.

On the way they stopped at Beersheba, where Jacob offered sacrifices to the God of his father Isaac.

God spoke to Jacob in a vision at night. "Jacob! Jacob!"

"Here I am!"

"I am the God of your father. Don't be afraid to go down to Egypt, for there I'll make your descendants into a great nation. I'll go down with you, and I'll bring your descendants back. You'll die in Egypt, and your son Joseph will be with you when you die."

They were a large group of people: Jacob and his eleven sons, their wives, all their children—seventy family members—their servants, and all their possessions.

Joseph ordered his chariot and went to Goshen to meet his father. As soon as he saw him, he threw his arms around him and cried for a long time.

Then Jacob said, "Now I'm ready to die, for I've seen your face and know that you're really alive."

Joseph took his brothers to the palace to meet Pharaoh. Pharaoh gave them permission to be shepherds in Goshen, and he asked them to look after his royal flocks. Goshen was located on rich delta land on the side of Egypt closest to Canaan. The soil was fertile, some of the best in Egypt.

Next Joseph brought his father to Pharaoh. The king spoke to the old man, and Jacob blessed him.

Then Joseph settled his family and gave them property in Goshen.

The famine got worse, but Joseph made sure that his family had enough food. He took over all the land in Egypt and saved the people from starving.

Jacob was an old, old man now, and he realized that he would soon die. He called Joseph to his bedside.

"If you wish to please me," he said, "promise not to bury me in Egypt. When I die, carry my body back to Canaan and bury me with my father and grandfather."

"I'll do just as you say," answered Joseph.

"Promise," said his father. And Joseph promised.

Then Jacob worshiped God right there in his bed.

Joseph brought his two sons, Manasseh and Ephraim, to their grandfather's bedside. Jacob pulled himself up to a sitting position on the bed.

"God Almighty appeared to me at Bethel, in the land of Canaan," he told Joseph. "He blessed me and promised to give me many descendants. He promised to give me that land for my descendants forever. I have twelve sons, but only two of you are the children of Rachel. Let me adopt your boys, who were born in Egypt, as my own, and let me count them as my sons."

Then the old man hugged and kissed Joseph's sons.

"I never expected to see your face again," he said to Joseph, "and here God has let me see your children, too!"

Then Joseph brought his boys close to Jacob, with Manasseh, the older one, on Jacob's right, and Ephraim, the younger one, on his left.

Jacob put out his hands to bless them, but he crossed his arms and put his right hand on Ephraim and his left hand on Manasseh.

Joseph tried to change his father's hands. "Not that way, Father! Here, put your right hand on the head of the firstborn!"

But Jacob wouldn't let him change his hands. "I know what I'm doing, my son. Manasseh will become a great tribe, but his younger brother will be greater."

Then he blessed Joseph's sons. "May these boys be blessed by the God of my fathers Abraham

164

and Isaac, the God who has been my shepherd all my life, the angel who has rescued me from all harm. May they have many descendants and may they keep the memory of their fathers' names alive!"

Then he said to Joseph, "I'm dying. But God will be with you and bring your descendants back to the land of your fathers."

Then Jacob called all his sons to his side and told them what would happen in the future. Each one would have many descendants, each one would be the ancestor of a tribe, and some day their descendants would return to the land that God had promised them.

He asked them to bury him in the cave of Machpelah, next to Abraham, Sarah, Isaac, Rebecca, and Leah.

When Jacob died, Joseph and his brothers carried his body back to Canaan and buried him beside his forefathers.

But when they returned to Egypt, Joseph's brothers were afraid. Now that their father was gone, would Joseph punish them? They sent Joseph a message, asking for his forgiveness. Joseph cried when he heard the message. Did they still not understand?

His brothers came to him, bowing down before him. "Let us be your slaves!" they said.

"Don't be afraid," he told them. "I'm not God. It's not up to me to punish you. Although you meant to hurt me, God made everything work out for good, and many people were saved from starvation. So don't worry. I'll take care of you and your families."

Joseph lived a long and full life after this. Many years later, as he lay dying, Joseph said to his brothers' families, "God will remember you and rescue you from this land. He'll lead you back to the land that he promised to Abraham, Isaac, and Jacob."

He asked them to make a promise. "When God brings your descendants out of Egypt, take my bones with you away from here."

Joseph died, and they embalmed his body, according to the Egyptian custom. They preserved it like a mummy so that it wouldn't decay, and they put it in a coffin. They didn't bury Joseph, but kept his body. They, and their children, and their grandchildren waited year after year for God to rescue them from Egypt and lead them back to the land of promise.